GOING GREAT GUNS

GOING GREAT GUNS

Arsenal from the Inside 1986-87

Kenny Sansom

To
Sarah
Be Lucky

K. Sansom

Macdonald
Queen Anne Press

A Queen Anne Press BOOK

First published in Great Britain in 1987 by
Queen Anne Press, a division of
Macdonald & Co (Publishers) Ltd
3rd Floor
Greater London House
Hampstead Road
London NW1 7QX

A BPCC plc Company

Jacket photographs
Bob Thomas Sports Photography

British Library Cataloguing in Publication Data

Sansom Kenny
Going Great Guns: inside Arsenal 1986-87
— (A Queen Anne Press Book).
1. Arsenal Football Club
I. Title
796.334'63'0924   GV943.6.A7
ISBN 0-356-15054-2

Typeset by York House Typographic Ltd, London W7
Printed and bound in Great Britain by
Butler & Tanner Ltd, Frome and London

CONTENTS

Colour photographs
Bob Thomas: World Cup; Steve Williams/Tony Grealish;
Viv Anderson/Ray Clemence; Charlie Nicholas/Ossie Ardiles;
Littlewoods Cup Final
All-Sport: Kenny Sansom/Wayne Clarke; Niall Quinn; Viv Anderson;
Kenny Sansom/Nico Claesen
Colorsport: David Rocastle/Arthur Albiston; David O'Leary

INTRODUCTION
BY BRIAN WOOLNOUGH

Before the start of the 1986 World Cup in Mexico, Kenny Sansom knew it was time to take a long hard look at his career. What had he achieved? Was he satisfied? Where was his life in football going? The answers that came into his head only emphasised the one thing that had bugged him since he first signed for Crystal Palace as a fifteen–year-old kid. He wasn't a winner!

As Sansom said goodbye to his wife Elaine and two young daughters before reporting for World Cup duty with the rest of the England squad, he thought a lot about winning. He was captain of Arsenal, one of the great club sides in world football, and England's first choice left-back approaching the fantastic landmark of 100 caps, but what did he have to show for years of dedication and consistency with club and country? Not much. He had won a Second Division Championship medal with Crystal Palace in 1979 and two *Daily Express* five-a-side competition winners' pennants, plus, of course, acclaim as one of the best left-backs in the world.

But that wasn't enough for the Camberwell-born player who had watched with envy as his international team-mates carried off all the top honours the game could offer. Sansom badly wanted to be a winner too. He wanted to get his hands on a trophy, he wanted to win the Championship with Arsenal, or climb up the steps at the end of a Wembley final and hold a cup aloft to a red and white sea of fans. He wanted to be proud of winning something and, with all due respect to Crystal Palace and the *Daily Express*, neither counted too much in his roll call of ambitions.

He had been at Highbury for six years, valued at a cool £1 million in August 1980, when he swopped clubs in the controversial transfer that took Clive Allen to Crystal Palace without kicking a ball for Arsenal. As an Arsenal player his reputation at international level grew; he played in the 1982 World Cup in Spain only to return disgusted that England should go out without losing a game.

That desire to succeed continued to haunt him as Arsenal, under manager Terry Neill and then Don Howe, just flirted with the major domestic prizes of English football. 'It drove me mad that I couldn't win anything' Sansom admits. 'I was the England left-back, captain of Arsenal and yet I just couldn't see myself winning a thing. In my first FA Cup tie for the club I put through my own goal at Everton and Arsenal were knocked out. As the frustration went on, it began to bug me.'

So in May 1986, Sansom, then 27 years old, set out on a journey with club and country to put the record straight. Another disappointing season with Arsenal behind him, he believed England could win the World Cup and hoped that Arsenal, under new management when he returned from Mexico, would finally give him the glory he desired. This is the story of that year – 'the greatest and most exciting year of my life' – and tells the tale of the agony, ecstasy and final heartbreak of the World Cup, and, at last, the joy of going to Wembley and winning the Littlewoods Cup with Arsenal. From the moment Sansom set off on his journey he jotted down day-by-day notes in a diary and this book reflects his thoughts and hopes of a year that is jampacked with the experiences of one of the top professionals in English football.

It begins inside the England dressing-room after the bitterness of going out of the World Cup to Maradona's handball goal and ends with Sansom recovering from a hernia operation, the most serious injury of his career. In between he describes the impact made at Highbury by new Arsenal manager George Graham, how a 22-match unbeaten run transformed their season, the joy of being a winner, the agony of playing on with his injury and the shock of Arsenal spending £350,000 on another left-back, Wimbledon's Nigel Winterburn, while he recovered from his operation at home.

'It is the greatest year of my life for many reasons' he says. 'I am a winner at last and that is the most important thing that has happened to me in a fantastic career. I also played some of the best football of my life until the stomach strain that turned out to be a hernia got me down. My wife Elaine also gave birth to our first son, Harry, born on Boxing Day, and that just completed the story of the year. What more could I ask for? And now I could retire a happy man. Any other winners' medals will be a bonus after this year.'

Sansom of course has no ambitions to quit the game he loves and desperately wants to win 100 England caps, perhaps even beat Bobby Moore's record of 108 en route to the 1988 European Championships in West Germany and the 1990 World Cup in Italy. Having tasted success and glory with Arsenal he also wants more top honours as captain of his club. 'If I reach all those goals I will go out of the game completely satisfied' he says. 'At international level I can't think any further than the next World Cup. There is no reason why I shouldn't carry on playing at the top level as long as my fitness remains intact.'

Sansom has been regarded as one of the world's best left-backs for years, his name up in lights in an era of exciting football alongside other great number threes like Briegel of West Germany, Italy's

Cabrini and new names such as the Argentinian Olarticoechea or the Russian Bessonov. Since he made his Arsenal debut against West Bromwich Albion on August 16 1980 and won his first England cap against Wales at Wembley in May 1979, Sansom has had no real challenger at club or international level. While he recovered from his hernia operation in May 1987 England capped Stuart Pearce of Nottingham Forest and brought Mitchell Thomas of Spurs into the squad without any suggestion from manager Bobby Robson that Sansom's era was coming to a close. Indeed, Sansom was the only left-back in Robson's squad for the Football League's encounter with the Rest of the World in August 1987.

There is one player however that Sansom knows could have halted his progress and even ruined his career at international level. Derek Statham and Sansom were early rivals when the West Bromwich Albion defender suffered a series of injuries. 'If I had to choose between us I would have to say that Derek was a better left-back than me' he admits honestly. 'Derek has been desperately unlucky with injury. Had he not suffered so badly I believe that he could have been England's left-back ahead of me. We would certainly have been in the England squad together and would still be rivals today. I feel sorry for him and my injury brought home to me how frustrating football can be when you can't play, or perform at your best. That said, I have never worried about the lack of competition and it has been flattering that for years the England manager has not even put a covering player for me in the England squad, not even when we went to Mexico.'

The arrival of George Graham as manager at Arsenal has seen the end of his unchallenged status at club level. Graham wants competition and the signing of Winterburn represented the first threat to Sansom since he arrived in 1980. It also came as a shock and there were hurried talks between captain and manager. Graham however insisted that he had no plans to discard Sansom and still regarded him as first choice and club captain. 'What angers me' says Graham 'is that Liverpool sign players and everyone accepts them as part of a big squad. I sign someone and everyone wants to know who is leaving. I want Arsenal to win everything but in my first season I discovered that the squad was not experienced enough. I didn't buy Winterburn to replace Sansom, I signed him to strengthen the squad. End of story.'

Graham then paid tribute to Sansom's role in an amazing first season for the new manager at Highbury. 'When I arrived I looked through the list of the playing staff and Kenny's name stuck out. Here was one of football's best players, someone with great standing in the game. Yet he had not fulfilled himself at club level. I had to ask myself, and him, "Why not?" Now I am delighted that he has got some recognition. He deserves it and I hope that it will be the first of many trophies he can lift for this club. The Littlewoods Cup should not have been the first trophy Kenny Sansom won. He knows that.

'When I was playing my last years of football at Crystal Palace, Kenny was just breaking through and we played in the same team at one stage. It gave me great pleasure ten years later to see him lift the cup at Wembley in my first year. He found the injury difficult to handle because it was the first real setback of his career. But I have told him that he is very much in my plans and he knows that Winterburn is only the first of many new faces to arrive at Arsenal. I want a squad big enough and good enough to take on the best. I want to win things.'

So does Sansom. He has waited too long to stop now. This book demonstrates how badly he wants to stay a winner!

Brian Woolnough

1

MEXICO '86 – THE END AND THE BEGINNING

The face at the dressing-room door was young and smiling. It was an Argentinian face but not one we recognised. If I had spoken their language I would have told him that he was not welcome. This was the England dressing-room at the Aztec Stadium in Mexico City on Sunday June 22 1986 and only minutes after we had gone out of the World Cup to Argentina by two goals to one; their first the now famous 'Hand of God' goal by Diego Maradona, the second the finest goal I have ever seen, by this same little man, known as the world's greatest player.

It was not Maradona's stupendous second goal, however, that created an atmosphere of bitterness and frustration, that built up anger and hostility in that dressing-room. It was the handball effort that instigated the swearing, cursing and demands for the match to be played again. Dressing-rooms are emotional places and this was as bitter as any I have known. Even so, the smiling kid was still in the doorway, offering us the shirts of the Argentinian players to exchange for our own. 'You can stick your shirts' I shouted. 'The game should be replayed.' Ted Croker, the Football Association Secretary was in the middle of the room trying to console us. There was more shouting, swearing and tears.

Ray Wilkins, a substitute for this game who knew all about frustration after being sent off against Morocco, finally looked at the shirts being passed around and realised that they were not even the match jerseys of the Argentinian team. 'We don't want these' he shouted at the face that was no longer smiling. The kid finally caught our mood and retreated without the presents he had come for. I don't believe any of the England players exchanged shirts, except Steve Hodge, who had run up to Maradona immediately the final whistle blew and got the best souvenir of his career. That was up to Hodgey. I don't believe I could have brought myself to do it, even if I had desperately wanted Maradona's blue and white striped shirt. He had cheated and we were out.

Realising you are out of the World Cup produces a feeling of absolute helplessness. The final whistle blows somewhere on the pitch and for a couple of seconds you just stand there and let a million thoughts wash over you. Opponents shake your hand; team-mates, some crying, others shouting, wander over and you look each other in the eye. There is no need for words, you are out. Another World Cup, another defeat, another chance of the biggest prize of any footballer's life gone.

Mexico was my second World Cup heartbreak. Four years earlier it had been Spain, when we went out after failing to score against either West Germany or Spain in our last matches. But Mexico was worse. I had played better, it was a stronger, more flexible squad of players. And deep down I had honestly believed that England had a great chance of winning the World Cup for only the second time in our history. We all know about the boys of '66. I wanted us to be the team of the '80s. I hate losing and this was the hardest pill I've ever had to swallow, perhaps because I felt that Mexico could be my last World Cup.

There were tears in the dressing-room and who can blame fully grown men for crying? We had been a family for 47 days; laughing, joking, sweating, swearing, training, playing and hoping as one. It is a build-up that prepares the mind and the body for the most important soccer tournament on earth. The closer the World Cup came the more we wanted to play. Then when it is all over all you want to do is get home. The flight is long but comfortable and there at Heathrow are Elaine and the kids. More tears, more emotion, more thinking of how it might have been but for bloody Maradona. I got lost trying to find the M25 out of Heathrow, the kids started to get irritable in the back seat and I thought 'Hell, where did the World Cup go?'

The planning that went on was so thorough, and then you lose so quickly. It seemed a long time since the 22 players selected by England manager Bobby Robson met up, all wearing our Football Association blazers and slacks, all happy and confident, certain that we could conquer the world.

Tuesday May 6

Elaine came into London with me for a final goodbye and we had a meal. Saying goodbye is always hard although this time it is balanced against the excitement of playing for your country in a World Cup. No one likes to be away from their family but for a professional footballer at the top of his career it is part and parcel of life. My mental build-up for Mexico had begun a few weeks earlier. As Arsenal's disappointing season wound down I began to dream ahead – this is not to be recommended but it is an inevitable reaction. Once or twice it crossed my mind that I might get injured and miss Mexico, although that fear never put me off my football. I have a good injury record and Bobby Robson paid me the compliment of not including another left-back in the squad.

Mexico and the problems of playing in South America had also been on our minds for some time. A year earlier we had gone to Mexico on tour to gain first-hand experience of the conditions, and in the weeks before we left this time FA doctor Vernon Edwards had reminded us of the do's and don'ts of the country. There had been never-ending injections against various diseases and a professor from Wales advised us on what to eat, or more importantly, what not to eat. Things like cornflakes, toast and jam were a must for breakfast and mid-day snacks while we were advised to stay away from the bacon, sausages and eggs.

Footballers, however, do not really worry about outside problems. We know we are being looked after in the best possible way; we stay in the best hotels, eat what we are given and, on reflection, I don't believe the preparation for the 1986 World Cup could have been any better. Bobby Robson and his backroom team did an excellent job.

The players met up early in the evening and we were all given our official clothes to wear, and other gear such as bags and holdalls. There was a Government reception in the evening where the Minister of Sport, Dick Tracey, wished us well and said good luck from the country. It brought home just how much the World Cup means to the public. We desperately wanted to do well and were certain that we were going to reach at least the final.

Wednesday May 7   We are on our way at last. The England party of players, management, Football Association officials and reporters flew to Colorado Springs for the start of our special altitude training. The scene which greeted us on arrival was typically American, with bright lights and neon signs everywhere in the airport. 'Have a nice day. Have a nice World Cup.' The journey to our hotel, the Broadmoor, took about 45 minutes and by the time we arrived the players were tired and ready for bed. It was a case of a hamburger and crashing out.

I always room with Glenn Hoddle of Tottenham on England trips. We are rivals on the pitch and good friends off it. Glenn and I had pictures of our family pinned above our beds all the time; it helps keep you going. This World Cup is not like Spain, it is so far away and you do feel cut off. The FA allow you a certain amount of money to 'phone home once a week although I did it most days. When footballers are away for long periods family friends respond superbly and Elaine was inundated with offers of help around the house. The boss likes to know if you have got any problems at home, if the kids are ill or anything like that. He would be annoyed if it began to affect you and he didn't know.

Thursday May 8   We woke up to snow, a sleety snow that fell all day and made our first 24 hours away from home depressing. The opening week is always the hardest and the longest. You are away from your family, away from your normal environment – I had never been anywhere like Colorado

Springs before. It was a day of exploring the hotel, taking a look at the training facilities and going for a walk to stretch the legs and start breathing exercises. No hard training yet, but where is the sun?

Friday May 9

Everyone except Dr Edwards went for a long walk, climbing up to 10,000 feet. We sat by a lake and enjoyed the view and the air. It was our first real experience of altitude and it felt good. A few of the lads were keen to run the boredom out of their system and so Glenn, Mark Hateley, Chris Waddle and I ran down the hill. We were like kids running in and out of the rocks and pools of water and Glenn was lucky to escape serious injury. He slipped on a wet rock and fell; we decided not to tell the boss.

When we got to the bottom we were hot and sweating although pleased to note that we recovered well, though next morning our thighs had tightened, a reminder that we had stretched muscles.

Saturday May 10

Cornflakes, toast and jam for breakfast with as much tea as you could drink and then off for our first day's training. It was only a warm-up with a five-a-side match, shooting and a few exercises. We trained for about 80 minutes and it was easy, but we knew worse was to come. Every day we had a sauna to clean the body and a steam bath to get used to the oppressive heat of Monterrey, where we were drawn for our first World Cup matches in Mexico. It is said to be the hottest corner of the country.

It was FA Cup final day at home, Liverpool versus Everton with Liverpool going for a League and Cup double. We were lazing around the pool when the match was on and a few of the lads kept us in touch with the score and scorers but we were not that bothered. I didn't feel involved sitting around the pool and waiting for the World Cup. We all felt relaxed and in the evening went to the cinema to watch *Police Academy Three*. There were no fans around and the Americans were not giving us any hassle. 'What is this man, are you a team?' The players are not interested in having a drink and that is a good sign of total commitment and professionalism.

Sunday May 11

Our first match since we left home. We played against the local air force base and beat them 11–0. It was an easy stroll although the lads took it seriously and showed that they really mean business. The commitment is there right throughout the squad; Glenn and I have started to do squats and sit-up exercises in our bedroom as extra training. We are determined to do well and believe we have a great chance. The feeling grows stronger as the trip continues.

Bryan Robson, our captain, didn't play in the game and the news-paper men are beginning to pick up stories that Pop isn't happy with his shoulder injury. It was touch and go whether he had an operation before the World Cup and there seemed to be doubts whether he is even going to play. The other players don't pin him down. We ask him how he is but we don't interview him. It is not worth taking a risk this early because Bryan is such a big influence on the side. He rooms with Ray Wilkins and there is not a better professional than Razor in the squad. He will not let Bryan get down and also gives him sound advice. The boss is obviously on top of the situation and has daily conversations with Bryan. It is worrying nevertheless.

Monday May 12

A day off. Swimming after breakfast, lunch and then a group of us played golf. Glenn won the tournament between 15 players and he and I beat Mark Hateley and Gary Stevens of Spurs in a pairs contest. Much to the delight of the others I fell out of the buggy going over a bridge at the 18th hole.

Glenn and I are really good mates. As always when you go away you become closer than at home. Try and make your room partner a real close friend at home and I don't believe it works. Back in London Glenn and I can go weeks without seeing each other but here we are laughing and joking and living under one roof for more than six weeks. Our friendship also means we have great understanding on the pitch. We know where each other wants the ball and we have a giggle during the match when things are going well. When Arsenal play Tottenham however that friendship is blanked out because we both want to win so badly.

Went to see *Back to the Future* in the evening, a great film. I had borrowed Glenn's copy of the book and read it all except the last two chapters – glad I didn't after going to see the film. What an ending!

Tuesday May 13

Back to training and it has started to get harder. We did a 660-yard test run because Dr Edwards wanted our pulse rate up to as near to 180 as we could get it. As we rested from the sprint he read our pulse every minute to see how quickly it took us to return to the resting rate of between 52 and 58. Most of us got down to 90 in five minutes and he seemed pleased. The more we sprinted the quicker the improvement. We had a game and practised shooting and corners. Bobby Robson is talking to us all the time although there are no real team meetings yet. The main concern is our physical condition, with the boss liaising with Dr Edwards all the time.

Overleaf: The England squad training against the spectacular backdrop of the Colorado Rockies. (Bob Thomas)

I am happy and the altitude conditions don't seem that much different. The boss just keeps us informed all the time, and no one struggles for fitness. Chris Waddle of Spurs doesn't look the fittest of footballers but he turns out to be head and shoulders above the rest of us. The only player who can get close to him is Gary Stevens of Everton.

Wednesday May 14

The end of our first week's preparation and we are all feeling great. My fitness is good and I am enjoying the training. The squad are relaxed,

another good sign. The routine is the same each day: breakfast between 8 and 10am, a couple of hours around the pool and then training, lunch and relaxation. The hotel is ideal for us; it's described as the gateway to the Colorado Rockies and offers a wide variety of recreational facilities which include 16 tennis courts and a 54-hole golf complex.

Today was slightly different however, as we played South Korea and beat them 4–1. I only played one half as the boss wanted to give Terry Fenwick a run at left-back in case anything should happen to me. It would be Fenwick who would play in my shirt during the World Cup if I was injured although Terry Butcher has also worn the number three jersey in his time, so we are well covered. I take it as a compliment that there is no second natural left-back in the squad. It is a good match watched by a large crowd.

When we return to the hotel Glenn is told that his manager at Spurs, Peter Shreeve, has been sacked and he is bitterly disappointed and upset. He and Shreeve are close and he believes that Tottenham have treated his friend very badly indeed. He goes straight to our room and tries to 'phone Shreeve at home. He can't get through after trying four times and says that Peter must have gone away for a few days with his family to escape from the hassle.

After our first week Glenn and I are £25 down on the World Cup card school. The England squad has a big card school and there are some compulsive players. Glenn and I are a pair, as are Bryan Robson and Ray Wilkins, Gary Bailey and Chris Woods, and Mark Hateley and Gary Stevens of Spurs – Peter Shilton always plays on his own. We are down and it looks as though Mark is ahead of the field at the moment. It has been a long day and after a walk across the other side of the local park and a couple of Budweisers the players are ready for bed.

Thursday May 15

Glenn has to go to the dentist. He is being troubled by a cap and is worried about going. Surprise surprise he gets no sympathy from anyone. I played John Barnes at tennis, lost 6–1 6–1 and thought I did well. John and Glenn are the best tennis players in the squad. Trained after lunch, took a sauna and steam bath and then went for a walk in the evening.

Friday May 16

Flew to Los Angeles for a game against Mexico and stayed at the University Hilton Inn Hotel. The previous night I had moved into a double room because when we return from LA the wives will be at the Broadmoor. We left Colorado at noon and arrived in Los Angeles at 5.30.

On the coach journey to the hotel Don Howe said he spotted a house without a swimming pool but no one believed him. Anyone who could spot one got a point; it sounds silly but it is the sort of game footballers play. We had dinner at 7pm and then watched the film *10* with Dudley Moore.

Saturday May 17

It is extremely hot and reminds me of the day in Spain when we kicked off in the 1982 World Cup in Bilbao. We have a team meeting after breakfast and then travel to play the Mexicans. It was a great game for us and a 3–0 win, with Mark Hateley (who scored two) and Peter Beardsley the goalscorers, provided the squad with a real boost. The longer the trip goes on the more confident everyone is becoming.

The only blackspot is the damn shoulder injury to Bryan Robson. During the game his shoulder pops out again and it is terrible to see Bryan down on the ground in agony. Fred Street, one of our trainers, puts the shoulder back in and that probably saved Bryan his World Cup place. Had the shoulder stayed out until he got to hospital it could have been sore and stiff and needed a longer recovery. It wasn't a bad dislocation, yet bad enough for England and our captain. Bobby Robson decided to keep the injury a secret. Bryan was under enough pressure without having to be the centre of another injury debate. Bryan walked out of the game and the lads are now worried that he will not make the first match against Portugal.

The match against the Mexicans went well and we played really confidently in the first half. Understandably because of the heat, we slowed down in the later stages and the Mexicans had some chances to score. I almost scored a rare goal. It was down to Glenn again, he knew where I was and I shot narrowly wide.

We were weighed before and after the game and I lost 8 lbs today. At half-time we were told to drink as much hot tea as possible and afterwards Dr Edwards just told us to drink as much fluid as possible, hot or cold. We also had urine samples taken every three days to test the salt levels in our bodies.

On the coach back to the hotel Gary Bailey and Steve Hodge took some terrible stick because we knew the wives and girlfriends were waiting and they were the only two players without ladies. 'We are OK tonight, lads, what will you be doing?'

Sunday May 18

I didn't sleep too well (which was not surprising). This was the start of 'ladies week' and the Football Association have to be congratulated and thanked for an impressive piece of public relations. They paid for the wives to fly out and stay with us and it proved to be a big success; it broke up the long period away from home and allowed the players to unwind totally.

Chris Waddle, Glenn and I went for a game of golf in the afternoon and the wives came along to caddy for us. They drove the buggies and seemed to enjoy themselves. Unfortunately Elaine, who is three months pregnant, didn't feel too well in the evening and we decided to

have dinner in our hotel room. Nice food, a bottle of white wine and talking about the kids, we could have been at home in Barnet.

Monday May 19

Bryan Robson is struggling although he tries not to let his real feelings affect the morale of the squad. He smiles but you know how he is feeling inside. It is a horrible situation for him and speculation is growing all the time. Will he go home to have an operation or will he stick it out and try and play? I believe he will still make it and pray that he does. This is not like playing for your club side, this is England and the World Cup. Injuries happen and you accept them at club level, but when it is the biggest event in the football world you only give in if you really have to. Bryan once missed a game at Wembley after being injured during the preparation. I can still see the disappointment etched in his face; multiply that by 1,000 and that is how he will feel if he has to miss the World Cup. It is ironic that for the second successive World Cup England's captain has struggled for fitness. In Spain Kevin Keegan suffered with a back injury and only came on as substitute against Spain in the last game when it was too late.

Gary Stevens (Spurs), Glenn, Chris Waddle and I and our wives went out for an Italian meal in the evening. I ordered spare ribs for a starter and a plateful that would have been too big for Fred Flintstone was put in front of me. There can't be any nightlife in Colorado because the waitresses started to hoover up around us at 9.15. Do you think they were telling us it was time to leave?

Tuesday May 20

We went training while the wives lazed by the pool. I am feeling superb, the fittest I have been for a long while. I have never felt happier with my form either and everything is geared to being 100 per cent right for the big kick-off.

The FA took us all out to dinner in the evening. They did this three times while the wives were with us and this proved another success. We all got dressed up in our official blazers and slacks, everyone that is except Steve Hodge. He must have the worst memory of anyone I have ever met. If we were told to wear leisure suits he came down in a blazer, if we said be ready at ten o'clock Hodgey appeared 15 minutes later. I told him that he forgets to forget.

Wednesday May 21

Gary Bailey, who has also been struggling with a knee injury, is finally passed fit and named in the official World Cup squad. It is a big relief for him as he has been training alone with Fred Street for most of the trip. There is a gymnasium in the hotel and Gary and Bryan Robson have been the most frequent visitors. When we train they stay out of the physical contact and just jog with Fred as he gives instructions and advice.

This is a day off but Glenn and I still do our own routine of exercises in our rooms. It is my daughter Natalie's sixth birthday on the 25th so

Opposite: Fore! Elaine doesn't seem too impressed . . .
(Bob Thomas)

Elaine and I go to the local shopping centre and buy her a nice gold bracelet that we have engraved.

Thursday May 22 Normal routine. Sunbathing, lunch and training. In the evening the FA take us all out again and there is an emotional scene with Dick Wragg, the chairman of the International Committee. Dick is the one-man social committee and all the wives show their gratitude by going across the room to him at the end of the meal and saying thanks. Bryan Robson's wife has to give a thankyou speech to the FA and worries about it throughout dinner. She handled it well.

Friday May 23 It is time for the wives to go home although it is the players who leave first as we head for Vancouver in Canada and the next leg of our marathon journey towards World Cup glory. Elaine had some trouble flying over because her passport has expired, and it needed the guy from Thomas Cook to persuade the customs people to let her through. She was worried about the return journey but everything was sorted out. We went for a walk and there were a few tears as we said goodbye. It was strange to see the faces of the wives disappear as we left for the airport on the coach but as soon as they were out of sight the card school started up again. That sounds terrible, but there was nothing we could do about it, and I believe it only proves the great team spirit between the lads.

We arrived at the Richmond Inn Hotel at 7pm and Bobby Robson named his team for the next day with Steve Hodge in for Bryan Robson. He said that he didn't want to take a chance with Pop and the pressure on the skipper is now intense. Questions are being asked by reporters and TV men every minute of the day and I admit that I have my doubts about Bryan making it. I thought the boss would have played him against Canada because surely it is best if he breaks down before the World Cup rather than in the opening game? It is obviously discussed at length between Bryan, the boss and the medical staff; they know best.

Saturday May 24 Canada made it hard for us. We won 1–0 (Mark Hateley scoring the winner) but they were fit and gave us some stick. I marked a lad called Paul who had trained at Arsenal only months before as he prepared for the World Cup. The worst part of the game for us came when Gary Lineker was helped off with a suspected fractured wrist. It looked bad because when players go down with an arm injury it is usually serious. Fortunately X-rays at a local hospital only showed severe bruising and Gary was allowed to carry on playing wearing a support on the wrist.

After lunch and a rest in the afternoon Glenn and I decided to go out for dinner and booked a table at a Chinese restaurant in Montreal. As we left our hotel to hail a taxi a total stranger approached us and asked if we would like a lift into town. We accepted the lift with reservations and our fears were justified when the driver began shouting out of his window to passers by, asking them if they knew where our restaurant was. It was an amazing scene, two English footballers dressed in their official tracksuits being driven around by a total stranger in a foreign country. I suppose we did take a massive security risk and anything could have happened. Fortunately 'our friend' turned out to be a genuine football fan. His name is Terry Kelly, an Irish solicitor from Montreal and a self-confessed football nut.

We never found the Chinese restaurant; instead we went to a place we had noticed earlier, with a revolving table that looked out over Vancouver. Mexico turned out to be Kelly's fifth World Cup and he revealed to us that he spends thousands of pounds travelling the world watching football, even visiting every one of our 91 League grounds. Apart from treating us he proved to be one of the funniest men I have ever met and entertained us all night with jokes and stories. We parted company the best of friends and when I returned from Mexico I received a Canadian magazine that featured an article on our new buddy and all his football travelling.

Sunday May 25

Off to Mexico at last and the flight to Monterrey turned out to be one of those plane nightmares that you dream about or watch at the cinema. Before we took off one of the other passengers noticed that his luggage was being left behind on the tarmac and he immediately insisted that he got off. 'I can't possibly fly on this aircraft,' he said and went back into the passenger terminal. I can't say that the players were worried at this stage, although we did notice that our skips were still on the tarmac along with the worried man's luggage.

The man's concern proved to be justified, however, and on the second part of the flight the plane started to run out of petrol. We were kept informed and there were a lot of worried faces as the plane began to lose speed and look for an unscheduled landing spot. You don't get many bad fliers amongst footballers but Chris Woods is one of the worst and as the plane slowed he cuddled up to Bryan Robson and tried to hide his eyes from what was going on around him. He was shaking and his fright rubbed off on a few of the other lads. The card school played on however, only stopping after a bumpy landing at an old air base in the middle of nowhere. As we came down I even joked to Glenn Hoddle, 'Here is the £50 I owe you!'

It proved to be a very long day and the players were exhausted by the time we arrived late at night at our headquarters at the Camino Real Hotel in Saltillo 50 miles outside Monterrey and 1,765 feet above sea level. The security for the England team was amazing – police cars followed us everywhere, armed guards stood nearby, a helicopter watched our every move and the hotel was like a fortress. It made you feel a mixture of excitement and importance. We had finally arrived at Mexico. The build-up was over, we were ready to prove ourselves.

Monday May 26

We treated training like a match routine. Physical work lasting 45 minutes, then a ten minute break and a match for the next 45 minutes. That got us used to the conditions in Mexico, and all the players were delighted that it didn't seem any more tiring than our training in Colorado. The only two players not to train with us were Gary Lineker, whose wrist is still in a cast and poor Bryan. They only trotted and sprinted with Fred Street. No one knows yet whether Pop is going to make it.

I lost 5lb in weight during the session and weighed in at 11st 1lb. That is lighter than normal for me and as I write this diary I am 12 st exactly. This is my normal weight and I am not a person who has to really watch what I eat. I usually have chips every day but footballers burn off the calories quickly and at Highbury we also have a sauna bath every other day.

Tuesday May 27

It is a real dilemma over Bryan Robson now. He is still training on his own and the pressmen are looking for headlines as the great day approaches. The boss and Bryan still don't know the answer to the big question everyone is asking – will the captain play against Portugal?

Everyone wants Bryan to play although I have no worries about the man who will come into the side. Steve Hodge, Pop's obvious replacement, is a quality player and will do a good job. There is also the argument that Glenn plays better when Bryan isn't in the team. Does he feel more responsible? Is he given a better role for his great talent? Do other players raise their game? These are all plausible explanations.

The Portugal game is really close now and there is a real buzz in the camp. The atmosphere is good and the players want to get down to the nitty gritty. If you have seen caged tigers waiting for meal time at the zoo, that is how we feel. We have prepared thoroughly and we are hungry for action.

Wednesday May 28

The hotel is superb and the waiters are really friendly. We have taught them cockney rhyming slang and they are now asking everyone if they want a cup of Rosie Lee, or announcing that Mr Robson is wanted on the Dog and Bone. I think they want us to win the World Cup more than their own team.

The Press are in the same hotel but there is no problem. There are a few news reporters around trying to dig up 'other stories' but they don't have any chance because all this England squad is interested in is winning the World Cup. We played Monterrey who were the Mexican champions and beat them 4–1. I didn't play in the first half and had a stiff back after the match ended. It could be the weight I have lost or the state of the pitch, which wasn't good. Three police cars accompanied us to and from the game.

Sitting on the touchline during the first half, I noticed that Dr Edwards looked really white and unwell. It was at this game that poor old Doc suffered his heart attack and was taken to hospital. I didn't see him helped away because I was playing but when I asked Fred Street after the game what had happened he told me that Doc had a problem and that there would be an announcement tomorrow.

There has been no mention of the Mexican earthquake that at one stage threatened the World Cup. Footballers are very insular when it comes to tournaments. They don't want outside distractions and the earthquake was not mentioned from the moment we arrived in Mexico to the day we left for home.

The headlines in the English papers say that Bryan Robson needs a miracle to be be fit for the Portugal match and the players have not been told.

Thursday May 29

We had to be out of the sun by 11.15 this morning – the closer the kick off gets the less sun we are allowed to have. Training however is stepped up, and we are still treating it like a match with a ten minute break in the middle of two 45 minute sessions. Glenn is very worried about the knee injury that is giving him trouble. He needs an ice-pack after training every day and probably won't risk running tomorrow. It won't keep him out of the team although Portugal is too close to take chances. His problems started in Colorado and he used to sit in our room then with an ice-pack on his knee.

The boss made an announcement about the Doc and it seems he is recovering. Get well soon Doc!

Bryan Robson didn't train with the team and I think Glenn will be the star of the World Cup, despite his knee worry.

Friday May 30

It rained hard and the training pitch was too waterlogged to use. We had our identity cards for the tournament made, more blood tests and everything is ready.

I spoke to Elaine on the telephone and she seemed fed up. Sent her some red roses for our anniversary on June 2. I arranged it through the ITV people and they sent me a bill of £14 when I got back from Mexico. I didn't mind, although you often do these TV people favours.

Saturday May 31

The last day of really tough training. It rained but we worked long and hard and a lot of work was done by Don Howe with the front players, Mark and Gary. They were ordered to close down defenders through-out the game and stop full-backs chasing forward. The session went on for ages. We knew it was the last day of concentrated training and it was a good feeling to know that the game was now just around the corner. Still no news about whether Bryan will make it.

Sunday June 1

At last, matches. We watched the opening World Cup game between Italy and Bulgaria along with a worldwide audience of 450 million in 142 countries. It ended 0–0 and the lads were not impressed. Matches

are on TV all the time now and it is good to see exactly what we are up against. The adrenalin is pumping and everyone wants to get going. There is absolutely no pressure on us and we feel great, really confident.

It was good to have Don Howe around. We have known each other well for a long time and I was sorry when he walked out on Arsenal last season. I was not surprised he did it however. A club like Arsenal should not go around approaching other managers (Terry Venables) while they still have one of the best in charge of the players. Don loves Arsenal and was bitterly disappointed at the way they acted. I believe Arsenal would like to say sorry but they can't – it is done now and the wounds are too deep to heal. Don is a man of principle and he had to resign.

I remember the day he walked out so well. He was very emotional when he came to tell the players what he had done and said: 'You won't realise what a great club this is until you leave it.' I think I will always remember that and it made me realise that it will take a very good offer to lure me away from Highbury.

He told us not to let the club down and to think of the fans and our team-mates. Don worked around the clock in an effort to make and create a great Arsenal side. He was bringing the youngsters through and perhaps his downfall was that he tried some of them too early. I often used to hear how Don stayed up until three in the morning studying videos and reading books in an effort to find something new and exciting for Arsenal. All he needed was a little bit of luck. I don't know whether to call him boss or Don these days. Ron Greenwood was the England manager in Spain in '82 and I still call him boss whenever I see him.

Bryan Robson, Ray Wilkins and Gary Stevens celebrate a goal against the Monterrey U-12 team, much to Bobby Robson's amusement.
(Bob Thomas)

2

RIDING THE ROLLER COASTER

Monday June 2

Bryan Robson will play in our opening match against Portugal. After all the worrying and speculation the boss has put Pop in and we all hope it isn't a gamble. A fit Bryan Robson is a first choice but there is no point in playing in the World Cup unless you are ready in body and mind. It is the team that everyone expected, the first choice and all the other players in the squad accept the situation. Deep down they knew that once Pop was pencilled in the side picked itself.

Tuesday June 3

England v Portugal at the Tecnologico Stadium, Monterrey. Team: Shilton, Stevens, Fenwick, Butcher, Sansom, Waddle, Wilkins, Hoddle, Robson, Hateley, Lineker.
Result: 0-1 Scorer: Carlos Manuel.
Travelling on the coach to the game there was an atmosphere of cool confidence. We thought we would win. We thought we were going to win the World Cup. We had trained on the pitch the day before and although not happy with the surface or the length of the grass nothing stopped us believing that Portugal would be brushed aside. I didn't know any of the Portugal players by name but we all knew their style.

As we approached the stadium my mind went back to England and my family, friends and the mass interest! It is always the same when English teams play in world competitions. When I am sitting at home watching big sporting events on television I want us to win badly. And, boy, did I want to win this one badly.

The game alas was bitterly disappointing. We just didn't play well and can't offer any excuses. Why? I don't know. We had prepared so well. Perhaps we were over prepared and had forgotten the football. We created chances in the first half only to miss them and it has to be said that Gary and Mark were disappointing up front. They just didn't function as a pair or individually. The message in the dressing-room at half-time was that if we played to our potential we would win. We were not despondent because we knew that we were the better team.

But we still forgot to play and then came the 75th minute mistake by me that resulted in the goal that will haunt me for the rest of my career.

The ball broke out to their right-winger Diamantino, a situation that I have faced a million times. 'This is easy, it's mine' I thought to myself and yet somehow he got around me. How, I still don't know. I have watched a video of my mistake twenty, thirty times and I still can't believe the fella beat me.

It seemed a long time before Terry Butcher came to cover me and the ball was slid across before we realised what was happening – and then it was in the net. I just couldn't believe it. It was a terrible goal for us to concede. My bad tackle, Butch was slow to react (probably because he is not used to me making mistakes) and then Fen and Gary Stevens were caught. It was a back four mistake and after the game we all held our hands up. In the dressing-room the boss said I made a 'poofy' tackle and he was right. It was just one of those days. Had we had a similar chance I don't believe we would have scored.

Back at the hotel I didn't say a lot. I was angry with myself and just told the reporters to blame me and leave me alone. I thought a lot over dinner although I didn't eat much. I thought about the preparation and wondered if we had played enough matches between ourselves. There just hadn't been the understanding there.

I should have nailed that fella. Tommy Smith, the former Liverpool tough guy, had a go at me in the *Sun* a few months later and said I was too much of a gentleman on the pitch. He said that I didn't tackle properly or kick; that is his opinion, but part of my game is that I don't like to give away free-kicks. I don't go steaming into tackles in case free-kicks are conceded. If the opposition scored a goal from one of my free-kicks I would blame myself.

I had a couple of beers and went to bed early. It was difficult to sleep and I kept asking the same question: 'Why didn't we play?'

Wednesday June 4

Got up to watch the Derby. Glenn and I were the bookmakers and everyone bet on the favourite, Dancing Brave. Only Martin Tyler of ITV came in on the winner, Shahrastani, and he only picked up £3. I used to be a bad, mad gambler and once blew thousands on the horses during my betting days. I admit now that there were times when I couldn't let a day go by without a trip to the bookies and seven years ago, when I was at Crystal Palace, I lost £800 in a day. There is no way I will make the same mistake again, and I have the drug under control now. Elaine and I might have the old flutter but that is all. I have learned my lesson and the responsibility of a young family has made me realise just how stupid I was. It got so bad at Palace that my manager, Terry Venables, advised me to go to Gamblers' Anonymous. I never did and managed to pull away from the betting shop myself and now I can see what a dangerous situation I was creating for myself.

We watched West Germany on the box and I can't wait to play again to get that mistake out of my system. The boss has told the Press that we can still win the Cup. That gave us all a big lift, we are still confident.

Thursday June 5

Did some training, talked about the next game against Morocco and the boss named the same team. I admit that we are all a bit nervous, a reaction to our defeat. But it can't go wrong again, can it?

Friday June 6

England v Morocco at the Tecnologico Stadium, Monterrey. Team: Shilton, Stevens, Fenwick, Butcher, Sansom, Waddle, Wilkins, Hoddle, Robson, Hateley, Lineker. Result: 0–0

For the first time in my career I wore boots with rubber studs. The pitch was hard but with a lot of grass and as some of the lads had used rubber in the first game I decided to give it a try. I took five pairs of boots to the World Cup, three pairs with studs and two with rubbers. Boots were always kept by Norman Medhurst who made sure that they were clean and in first class condition.

The first half was a living hell, the most sickening 45 minutes I have played in during my career. The nightmare began when Bryan Robson went down from a tackle in the penalty box and injured his shoulder again. As soon as he went down we heard something go and Bryan cry out and we knew that was the end of the World Cup for him. I looked at poor Pop on the ground and my heart went out to him. There is nothing worse, nothing more sickening than being injured in a big competition. Was he right to play in the first place? Bryan felt he was OK, the boss wanted him in the side and the rest of the players were right behind that decision.

If that was bad enough worse was to follow. Ray Wilkins threw the ball down in frustration at a decision by referee Gonzales and the Paraguayan official sent Ray off. I don't believe Ray should have been sent off and he insisted that he didn't throw the ball at the referee, which was said to be the reason for his dismissal. He is very close to Bryan, perhaps his frustration and feelings for his mate spilled over in that split second without him even realising.

I thought it was a harsh decision, and as Ray walked off I believed our chances of going any further in the 1986 World Cup went with him. I thought we were going to be beaten because Morocco had been a useful side and I thought they would take us in the second half. The dressing-room was a terrible place to be at half-time. Ray sat in the corner saying he just couldn't believe what was happening. 'It is a dream, it just can't happen' he said over and over again.

We just had to pick ourselves off the floor and amazingly, Morocco started to back off in the second half. They seemed to be happy with a draw against England and the more they retreated the more confident we became. We were so determined and they seemed scared to us – we could even have sneaked an amazing victory.

That second half changed the mood of the camp. From despair we suddenly believed that all was not lost. We had played well in the second half and drew on everything we could muster to bring us up to a level of confidence that would shock Poland, the match that would make or break our World Cup.

Saturday June 7

The inquest. It wasn't a happy bunch of players who sat in front of Bobby Robson and Don Howe and desperately tried to work out what had gone wrong. We knew everyone in England was asking the question but we couldn't really find the answers. Had we overtrained, had we played enough football as a team, were we over confident? Each time I told myself 'no' without ever feeling convinced. One thing was sure, we were not scoring goals and that was a big worry.

The boss had a blackboard behind him as he spoke and suddenly he turned over a large piece of paper and there were our alternatives as this World Cup reached the crossroads. Depending on how we did against Poland in our make-or-break match we would either go on to Mexico City or Guadalajara or get on the plane back to Heathrow. It was as simple as that.

The boss is under tremendous pressure from the media. They are calling us flops and him a failure. That drives the players on and we are all convinced that we can beat Poland. We can, can't we? The boss is more uptight than at any time of the trip so far. If the players do anything wrong or step out of line I am sure he will jump on us. It was a day to get away from the pressure of the situation. Most of us left the hotel and the media behind and went up into the hills to laze in the sunshine and play cricket. Someone produced a tape recorder for some music and later in the day we had a barbecue. I have to say at this stage that we are all worried that we are going out in disgrace.

Sunday June 8

We trained but it wasn't hard. I try to take my mind off the match against Poland but whatever the team does we can't help thinking about the outcome of one of the most important matches of our lives. There is speculation that 0–0 will be good enough but that is out of the question for the players. We are going for the win, yet where are the goals coming from? I am having a slight problem with an ankle injury and don't think I will train tomorrow. It won't keep me out of the game however. No way.

Monday June 9

There is a growing feeling that the Press and a lot of people back home are blaming Don Howe for England's lack of success, and goals. Don has always had his critics and for some reason is called a negative coach and I would like to take this opportunity to put the record straight.

Don was my coach and manager at Arsenal and has been with England under Ron Greenwood and now Bobby Robson. In all those years he has never tried to make any team I have played in defensive.

He has encouraged me to overlap and attack and has never attempted to prevent 'flair' players doing what they are good at.

Like all successful managers and coaches he doesn't like to give goals away and works hard at making the defence a watertight organisation. There is nothing wrong with that and it was George Graham's priority the moment he took over at Highbury from Don. I think it is about time that the critics got off Don's back and tried to find other reasons for failure. The easiest thing in the world is to blame Don when they don't really know what they are talking about.

With England Don does most of the warm-ups but it is the boss who dictates the tactics. Bobby is the England coach, don't make any mistake about that. He joins in the training matches and five-a-sides and often stops play to put over his points of view. Don is involved as well but Bobby does the coaching. He enjoys the five-a-sides and during the World Cup caught me with a real over-the-top tackle and gashed my leg.

Tuesday June 10

The team is announced and there are a lot of changes. Both Ray Wilkins, who is suspended, and Bryan Robson, out with his injury, can't play and they are replaced by Peter Reid and Steve Hodge. The boss also drops Chris Waddle and brings in Trevor Steven of Everton. Perhaps his most significant change is calling up Peter Beardsley and dropping Hateley. Mark is bitterly disappointed and the boss had obviously told him before the team meeting because when the side is announced Mark doesn't appear too shocked. I felt sorry for him although he would be the first to admit that he hasn't done himself justice so far. We are not scoring goals and something had to be done. The boss has gone from Mark's height and power to the more subtle approach of Peter.

I am pleased Peter Reid is in. He is a player who gets others operating and I believe complements Glenn Hoddle well. Reid doesn't allow the opposition to settle and gets the game played at this own pace. We call him 'The General'.

Well that is it, the team that simply must not let England down. I go to bed knowing that by this time tomorrow everyone in England will be in mourning or alive again in the land of hope. I go to sleep desperate to wake up and for the match to kick off.

Wednesday June 11

England v Poland at the Universitario Stadium, Monterrey. Team: Shilton, the new captain, Stevens, Fenwick, Butcher, Sansom, Steven, Hoddle, Reid, Hodge, Lineker, Beardsley.
Result: 3–0 Scorer: Lineker (3)
We hammer them in the first 20 minutes and a feeling of relief and excitement washes over the entire England camp. As soon as Gary Lineker scores the first goal of his hat-trick, the players begin to look like their old selves. Confidence and expression comes flooding back.

The funny thing is that Poland could have scored before we did. Terry Fenwick made a mistake, probably due to the nerves of the situation, and I don't know what effect an early goal against us would have had on the side. I didn't get much time to ponder on that because Gary completed his hat-trick before half-time and you can imagine the mood in the dressing-room. We knew, at last, we were doing ourselves justice.

The goal that changed our World Cup – Gary Lineker's first against Poland.
(Bob Thomas)

There is no question that we could have scored more goals because Poland were a bad side, worse than Portugal and Morocco, which completely contradicted our World Cup planning. Gary looked razor sharp and it is amazing what a goal does for a striker. Three in one game makes him believe he can score in every match!

However, our message after the game was 'Don't get carried away.' We have only just begun. And it has been a bloody long time coming. The boss must take a lot of credit for our revival. Through the miserable times he kept his own head and that helped us keep ours. He kept telling us 'If I go down, so will you.' He made a big point about the fans back home and how proud they wanted to be of the England side. 'Do you want to let your country down?' he asked us over and over again. To lose in the World Cup to the big countries like Brazil is just about OK, but it would have been sickening to go out after being put in a group with smaller footballing nations like Portugal, Morocco and Poland.

The drinks flowed after the game. The players wanted to unwind and everyone had a few beers. My mum Rose and an uncle and his wife came to the hotel for dinner and at last the mind was relaxed. The tension had gone but not for long, because Mexico City and Paraguay were just around the corner.

Thursday June 12

A story is breaking that Barcelona and their manager Terry Venables want Gary Lineker and that they are prepared to pay more than £2 million. This is not a surprise to the players as the rumours were circulating daily when we were in Colorado Springs. When we ask Gary he is clearly embarrassed and we know that it is true, although he wants to keep it quiet until after the World Cup. As part of our preparation for our meeting with Paraguay in the next round, we all visited a monastery in the hills to help acclimatise for Mexico City which is 7,000 feet above sea level.

Friday June 13

Flew to Mexico City and booked into the Holiday Inn Hotel. The main game of the day was Scotland versus Uruguay, with our great rivals from north of the border needing to win to stay in the competition. There is fierce rivalry between Scotland and England and although we didn't want to see them beaten, deep down all the England players were delighted that the Jocks only drew and went out. We didn't want them staying in longer than us.

The Delvalle Hotel was very disappointing. It was extremely noisy, the food poor and our room smelled. Glenn used up four cans of Brut in an effort to lift the pong and also sprayed the sheets. We found it difficult to sleep and it was no surprise when the England party switched to the Holiday Inn.

Bryan Robson is clearly extremely depressed at being injured and out of the team and there is even talk of him going home. But he wants to stay and never lets his true feelings filter through to the rest of the team. Training is now just about free kicks and tactics. Suddenly we all believe that we can win the World Cup again although we know that tough teams are ahead. Don't get carried away!

Saturday June 14

Terry Butcher travelled to the World Cup with his future with Ipswich in doubt and a number of big clubs are interested, including Spurs, Manchester United and Glasgow Rangers. Big Butch however refuses to discuss anything but the World Cup with reporters and I don't blame them for not pushing him! He is a 'big un'. Terry and Shilts have minor injuries but neither of them will miss the game.

Sunday June 15

We know that if we beat Paraguay we will face Argentina and that means incredible pressure on and off the field. It will be the first time the two countries have met since the Falklands War and the questions are already being asked by the Press. The players however are not interested in anything but football.

Monday June 16

We trained at the Aztec Stadium for the first time and it is not as good as last year when we were on tour. Must not let that worry us. The team picked itself and after Poland all the other players knew that with one exception it had to be the same side. What would have happened had Bryan not been injured or Ray been sent off? Would the team have been changed anyway? Who knows? There was one enforced change with Alvin Martin coming into the side in the middle of the defence in place of Terry Fenwick, who had collected two cautions and a one-match suspension.

Tuesday June 17

Training was again all about tactics and dead-ball situations. There is a different altitude in Mexico City and we are reminded of this in all the training we do. The preparation is spot on again and the players are confident. We have the same feeling back in the camp as before the opening match.

Dr Edwards is better, but unable to carry on his duties with the squad and my club doc, Alan Crane, is flown out to join us in Mexico City.

Wednesday June 18

England v Paraguay in the Aztec Stadium, Mexico City. Team: Shilton, Stevens, Martin, Butcher, Sansom, Steven, Hoddle, Reid, Hodge, Lineker, Beardsley.
Result: 3–0 Scorers: Lineker 2, Beardsley.
We are not so nervous before the game and that is a good sign. I am confident we are going to beat them. There is no better bunch of people than the English when the chips are down and our strength has been cemented through the bad results. We stuck together as a unit and that showed right the way through.

I wore studs again as the pitch was slippery and the fella I was marking was quite quick. We started so confidently and knocked them out of their stride with goals. They began moaning and groaning and went mad with the referee when the score was 2–0 and he turned down what they thought was a penalty. It began to get physical and there were boots and elbows flying around. Once we got in front however they were never in it and it is easy to walk away from trouble and stay cool when you are winning.

All the frustration was on their side and Gary helped himself to another two goals. I was delighted that Peter Beardsley also scored; in his two matches he has done so much unselfish running and work. Gary is buzzing and has a chance to finish as the World Cup's top goal-scorer. Who'd have predicted that after our opening two matches?

You can imagine the mood after the game. We can win the World Cup – again. The players are on a high, everything is alright once more. We can play, we can score goals, we are going to beat Argentina in the quarter-final.

Thursday June 19

The game against Argentina is four days away and the build-up is quite incredible. I 'phone home and Elaine tells me that everyone is talking about the Falklands. That is furthest from the players' minds, and I wish that we could have played Argentina later than the quarter-final.

I had played against them and the great Diego Maradona once before at Wembley in May 1980 and had an old score to settle. He beat me on one of his exciting dribbles and I tripped him in the area and they scored from the penalty. We still beat them 3–1 and I quickly entered in my World Cup diary: 'I hope the score is the same'.

The boss called a team meeting and told us to forget about the Falklands and banned us from discussing it in interviews with the media. Not that we needed reminding.

Friday June 20

I am a firm believer in taking the rough with the smooth as far as the Press goes. They have a job to do and unless they go right over the top I let criticism ride. Some of the other players react and the strikers, who are the players who always get the big publicity, can be particularly hurt. The Press are now saying nice things about the team again and some of the players want to remind them of articles written when the results were disappointing. I remember what was written but never let it upset me. Being a defender is easier, not like it is for Glenn or Gary. They are always in the spotlight.

Saturday June 21

Maradona is on everyone's lips. Will we man-to-man mark him? How highly do we rate him? Is he the best? Are we worried about him? Are we scared of him? The answer is probably best given by the fact that no one was detailed to mark him individually. We were told that if he came into our zone the appropriate person should pick him up. That was fine by me although I would have been happy to man mark him if that was what Bobby Robson had wanted. I was asked the question by a reporter before the game, and as I am the same height and size as Maradona I suppose it was a fair question. I said that I would give it a go but the boss didn't want anyone worrying about one certain opponent.

I was free of nerves. We knew that Maradona was a danger but didn't believe he was good enough to beat us on his own. We didn't watch videos of Argentina or Maradona as that can often leave you blinded by science. We were confident, let them worry about us. I went to bed certain that we would beat them. The boss brought back Terry Fenwick, now free of suspension, in place of a bitterly disappointed Alvin Martin. So it was the team that beat Poland, a good omen perhaps.

Sunday June 22   England v Argentina. Aztec Stadium, Mexico City. Team: Shilton, Stevens, Fenwick, Butcher, Sansom, Steven, Hoddle, Reid, Hodge, Lineker, Beardsley.
Result: 1–2 Scorer: Lineker.
This is the big one, the moment of truth for England. The day when all the planning, training, sweating and swearing fuses into one. It is the point of no return for a lot of the team. We know that a mistake will be the end of our World Cup dreams, not just for this year but, for some of us, for ever. It is that feeling that pumps through your body when you line up to go out. Hands are shaken, backs are slapped, although you don't really notice individuals or remember what they say. All you want to do is get through that door and win.

The talk has been of Maradona and the Falklands but, hell, he is only one player. We know he is the greatest player on earth today but Argentina must be worried about us too. They can't be pleased that Gary Lineker has struck goalscoring form and we are full of confidence. There are more nerves than normal. It is a big occasion and it has definitely got to one or two of the lads. Suddenly you are out in the heat and the wall of noise and colour is screaming down at you. Is that Maradona? Who is that one? Oh hell, what does it matter?

The kick-off and more fists shaken in anger, tension released and nerves. We are hyped up and it definitely affects our first half performance. On reflection I believe we lost the match in the opening 45 minutes. We didn't play, we didn't allow ourselves time to settle.

Half-time and the talk is of relaxing , calming the play down. We are still confident because they don't really look like scoring. Do we? I can't really remember.

And then a goal for Argentina, a controversial goal out of nothing. And it had to be him. Maradona's 'Hand of God' goal will go down as one of the most controversial in the history of football. At the time I didn't see him handle because I was looking away at other Argentinian players making runs into open space. But as soon as I heard the rest of the lads shout handball and saw Shilts sprint to the halfway line I knew the goal should not have been allowed.

I have never seen Peter Shilton move so quickly and all the players joined in the protest. No one could believe that the referee and the linesman had not seen the incident. I have since watched it hundreds of times on video and it is so clear, and I also have a massive picture in my home to remind me of the goal that probably cost me a World Cup winners' medal. The picture is clear. Maradona with his arm raised, fist clenched and his eyes shut tight together. Why didn't referee

Diego Maradona applies the finishing touch to the greatest goal I have ever seen (Bob Thomas)

Bennaceur of Tunisia see it? That will always remain one of the unanswered questions of the World Cup.

I have no doubt in my mind that Maradona meant to do it. His eyes were closed because he knew he might get clattered by Shilts and he just gambled and got away with it. Is he a cheat? Yes, probably. Would we have been delighted to get away with a similar goal and reach the semi-finals? Yes, definitely. Maradona has since admitted that he handled the ball and I wonder what would have happened if the referee had asked him on the spot. Would he have said yes then? I doubt it. It would have taken a big man to do it.

It is easy to be wise after the event but I believe I would have confessed if I had been placed in a similar position. The goal was so important, the occasion so big you had to appreciate that it would get worldwide coverage. There was no way you could hide from an incident like that, television and newspapers would show the truth. He had to admit it when the evidence was produced and I believe he should have owned up out there on the pitch. There is also no doubt in my mind that the goal played on Maradona's conscience the longer the game went on. He knew he couldn't let that goal win the game, and soon produced one of the greatest goals I have ever seen. It was his way of ending the argument perhaps and there was certainly no dispute over this one.

I had a great view of him after going on a run down our left. The move broke down and I turned to see Maradona start accelerating towards our goal. Past one he went, then another and before anyone could do anything about it the ball was in the net. If his first was the hand of God, this was the hand of a genius. You can't blame defenders for the goal, he was so quick, so skilful, so deadly. A lot of people have since said to me that he should have been fouled and brought down. That is easier said than done when you believe you can win the ball and are beaten with pure skill. He went around Terry Butcher as if he wasn't there.

Our reaction after the first goal was one of anger and a realisation that we had to score a goal to get back into the game. Now we knew we were right up against it, probably going out. That doesn't flash before your eyes, you still try and remain calm and play the football that has been taught to you. 'Keep playing' was the cry. 'We can still do it'. But did we really believe that?

In the first half we had been frightened of them. Argentina had a young side and yet it was us who seemed to be reacting badly. I am certain that had Maradona not been in their side our attitude would have been different, we would have played better and probably won. Amazingly, we played our best football when 2–0 down. The English spirit came pumping through and after Gary scored they became frightened of us. Why did we leave this so late, why does it go wrong when it really matters?

Then the final whistle and the rest is a blur. Cameras, fans, noise, tears, swearing, handshakes and the sudden realisation that England are out. In a matter of seconds you think of many things, your family, going home and then you find yourself in the middle of a bitter dressing-room. Shirts are thrown, some players shout, others cry while some just sit in the corner with their head in their hands. Bobby Robson and Don Howe are quiet, their disappointment is as strong as ours. I was swearing, using every word I could think of. It was a release of frustration and bitter disappointment. Then the face at the door appeared and everyone could have hit that smiling face.

My mood turned to tears later when I rang home and heard Elaine's voice down the other end of the telephone. 'I'll see you in a couple of days,' I said and when the 'phone was put down so closed another World Cup. It's over, finished, let's just get the hell out of here. That night I did exactly what I did in Spain after we had gone out of the 1982 World Cup following a feeble goalless draw with the host nation. I had a right few drinks, visited a club and woke up with a hangover. It is difficult to sleep because all you can imagine is Maradona's hand going up, up, up above Shilton and then the little master turning away in glory after his second goal. Then that damn smiling face again!

When I retire I will never forget Maradona. He is a fantastic player, so quick, so strong. He is not big, but wide and powerful and once when he ran into me during the game his head hit my stomach and I thought I had been hit by a runaway bull. Sometimes I watch him and get annoyed because he could do so much more. The other disappointing part of his game is that he goes down too easily. I know that he is the target of a lot of hatchet defenders around the world but you lose respect if you collapse in agony when you are not hurt.

When I watched the Argentinians in the semi-final and final I thought they became arrogant and big headed and I can't stand that kind of behaviour. Suddenly it was easy to see how Ray got sent off. I certainly don't believe that Argentina were the best side in Mexico. They are the the world champions but for me Brazil and France were the outstanding teams, and I would have loved to see Brazil in the final. I believe they would have won it.

The last word on our defeat by Argentina goes for Peter Shilton. Shilts has received a lot of criticism for the first goal with many people saying that he should have clattered Maradona and knocked him back towards the halfway line. He certainly wasn't blamed for the goal by Robson or any of the team and I have to say that Shilts was just as sound, as commanding in Mexico as he was in Spain. I didn't spot any differences in his goalkeeping.

He received a lot of stick in the 1986–87 season with people like Wimbledon manager Dave Bassett saying that he was suspect on crosses. It's funny but I have never thought that Peter was outstanding on crosses. He certainly doesn't come for them like the Coventry goalkeeper Steve Ogrizovic. He is just a great goalkeeper, a magnificent shot-stopper and a good organiser. He will be around for a few internationals yet and I hope that he gets his 100 caps. I do believe, however, that the World Cup took a lot out of him.

By the time we arrived back at Heathrow I was ready for home and then a holiday. We had been away a long time; it is great while you are playing and praying but once you are out you relax, unwind and want to be with your family and away from the strains and pressure. We went to Portugal for our holiday soon after I got back and it was good to just sunbathe, swim and play with the kids. At the back of my mind were Arsenal and new manager George Graham but that could wait.

World Cup postscript   I enjoyed Mexico more than Spain. I was fitter, played better and didn't feel so disappointed after we went out. Spain was terrible because we didn't score goals against West Germany and Spain when it mattered and came home without even being beaten. At least with Mexico we can look at the record books and see Argentina 2 England 1, even if the first was a disputed goal, and even though we didn't play well until 2–0 down.

I have never been away with a happier, nicer bunch of players. We all got on well and that reflects good management. There may be better managers and coaches in the world than Bobby Robson, yet he has got the respect of the players because he is a nice man and that is very important. You can also trust him, a vital quality in a manager. If you are a manager and lose the respect of the players you are dead.

Bobby Robson wants to succeed so much he can get up players' noses by doing stupid things and saying things he probably doesn't really mean. But he is a players' manager and we can have no real complaints. He had his critics and the knives were out for him when things were going wrong in Mexico. The Football Association, however, like and respect him and it was no surprise to me when he was offered another five-year contract. OK, England have not won anything under him but when you look around, who is there better equipped to take over?

Terry Venables is the popular choice and there is no bigger admirer of Venners than me. He was my manager and coach at Crystal Palace and I rate him very highly. Had he been here and not in Barcelona I believe it would have been a different story. The FA would have been under incredible pressure to move him into Lancaster Gate and get rid of Robson.

Throughout the World Cup and its build-up Robson gave the players little sayings that we had to remember and repeat throughout the tournament. It was done to stamp thoughts in players' minds. Mine was: 'Don't pass him over, hand him over', – a reference to my understanding with Terry Butcher. Don't let a player wander across defence, hand him to Butcher with instructions was the meaning.

Many of the other players were given similar instructions:
Viv Anderson: 'Follow up both ends, shots and penalties.'
Peter Beardsley: 'An early shout sorts it out.'
Terry Butcher: 'Win the first header, if not the second – in both boxes.'
Glenn Hoddle's was the most hilarious and even the boss forgot it: 'When in possession, you can be out of position, when out of possession, make sure you are in position.'

Glenn and I also gave the squad nicknames; some are obvious and the others I will leave to your imagination:
Bobby Robson: I can't repeat most of them although 'Rick' was a favourite. He was always making mistakes with names. He would call me Kenny Statham. At the airport once he picked up a bag and went looking for Peter Reid even though Peter wasn't with the party.
Don Howe: 'Chuck' because our coach driver in Colorado had no hair and was called Chuck.
Peter Shilton: 'Shilly'. He told us about a golf day with Southampton and how he had hit a bad tee–shot and the local paper christened him 'Silly Shilly'. He wished he hadn't mentioned the story by the end of the trip.
Viv Anderson: 'Busy' because he never stopped talking.
Gary Stevens and Trevor Steven: 'The Hustlers' because they were never off the pool table.
Glenn and me: 'The Blues Brothers'.
Mark Hateley: 'Psycho'.
Bryan Robson: 'Pop'.
Chris Waddle: 'Barry Norman' because he knows every film, who is in it and where it is on.
Peter Beardsley: 'Ceefax' because Peter knows everything on television, the time and channel.
Steve Hodge: 'Forgetful'. Even Bobby Robson said 'Put a tag on him at the airport in case we lose him.'
John Barnes: 'Digger'.
Peter Reid: 'Freddie Starr'.
Gary Lineker: 'Hero'.
I mention these names as an example of the great friendship and camaraderie in the squad. It was a happy trip with no incident outside football to put the pressure on. Bryan Robson's injury was damn bad luck while Ray Wilkins' sending off was unfortunate. Our bad start was more disappointing for the players than you can imagine and I often wonder what the reaction of the Press and public would have been had we started and finished in disaster.

I thoroughly enjoyed the World Cup. My fitness was excellent, my form good and I enjoyed the experience once again of playing in a tournament along with the greatest players you can name. I regard myself as very lucky to have played in two World Cups and the only regret is that we didn't do ourselves justice in Spain or Mexico for different reasons. I am a winner by nature, I hate losing and can't stand anyone who doesn't give 100 per cent.

Going out in Spain, failing to score in our last two matches, was unforgivable while in Mexico we were so near, and yet, so far. I also believe that Mexico could be my last World Cup. I can't think beyond the 1988 European Championships in West Germany, certainly not to Italy 1990. I will be pleased to remain a member of the side in Germany and anything after that will be a bonus. I would dearly love to get 100 England caps although I think it might just be beyond me. I will give it everything I have got but when a player gets to 31 and 32 he should be coming to the end of his international career.

Mexico certainly made a bigger impression on me than Spain. It broadened my horizons as a player and a person and I returned home believing that I would like to leave Arsenal and play abroad in Europe. I didn't want to leave Arsenal and yet something told me that it could be the time to go. At 27 I was playing the best football of my career and if I didn't make the break I never would.

It was in my thoughts when I relaxed on holiday and at the back of my mind when I returned for pre-season training at London Colney, Arsenal's training ground in Hertfordshire. I never got around to discussing my future with new Arsenal manager George Graham and, as things worked out, I am delighted I didn't. I soon forgot all about the idea of leaving Highbury.

3

BACK TO WORK – GEORGE GRAHAM STYLE

I was in Colorado with England when I first heard that George Graham was the new manager of Arsenal. George had been a member of the Arsenal side that did the FA Cup and First Division Championship double in 1970–71; he had then gone on to work with his good friend Terry Venables at Crystal Palace and Queen's Park Rangers as youth team manager before being appointed manager of Millwall. We knew each other fairly well as he and his family live close to us in New Barnet on the outskirts of London.

Terry Fenwick was the first player to give me the lowdown on George and one night in Colorado took great delight in telling me what a tough disciplinarian my new boss could be. Terry, however, only played for Graham as a youth team player and it is different with kids – you have to be hard.

It was a coincidence that George should be my new manager because shortly before the World Cup we had bumped into each other in a local wine bar and had a long discussion about our thoughts and hopes for the game. I accused him of being too negative and defensive and said his teams should attack more. He told me that he liked his sides to have good shape and added that I seemed frustrated. George said that all my talk of getting players forward indicated that I wanted to win things. I replied that I was desperate to get my hand on a trophy because I had never won anything in my life. It was strange that I should be telling him about attacking and winning and then, suddenly, George was my manager. And it was a funny feeling being in Colorado with seven weeks to wait before meeting my new club boss. I just had to put him and Arsenal to the back of my mind and get on with more important things, like preparing for the World Cup.

George wanted all the Arsenal players back on July 16 for pre-season training and I had to contact him, explain that my Portugal holiday didn't end until the 17th and ask if I could report a few days late. He said that was fine and so Viv Anderson, Arsenal's other member of the World Cup squad, and I turned up at Colney a few days later than the rest of the Arsenal players.

As soon as I arrived at the training ground he greeted me and I said

'Hello, George'. The reply was quick and to the point. 'Don't call me George, it's boss from now on.' He then pulled me aside and explained that if it was in the local wine bar George was fine but on Arsenal business or at Highbury or Colney he wanted to be called boss. 'Fair enough', I thought. In fact, I like to call my managers boss.

The first weeks of training were nothing hard, but significant in the way the boss stamped his personality and character on the players. If a player kicked a ball away, even in a warm-up, he was told to go and retrieve it. If he said, 'It's OK, I'll get it later,' the reply again was stern and straight to the point. 'No, go and get it now,' and the game or training session didn't continue until the player, a junior or first team star, went and got the ball.

It was George Graham's way of gaining respect. It built slowly and we all realised that here was a man of his word. You also knew that you didn't mess with the new Arsenal manager. Perhaps Terry Fenwick had been right after all. It didn't take me long to realise that George Graham had been greatly influenced by Terry Venables. Things he said, things he did, were similar.

In one of the first squad talks the boss gave he told us his hopes for Arsenal. He wanted to make them great again, regain the reputation that the club had in the 70s under Bertie Mee. Respect and fear were the key words: he wanted the rest of football to worry about playing Arsenal once more. He also warned us that it was going to be a slow process. 'It is going to take time,' he told us. 'But between us we can do it.' All the Arsenal players were thinking the same standing in front of George Graham. 'I wonder how long it will take this manager to win something big for Arsenal?'

Tuesday July 22

There is a great deal of sussing out on and off the pitch when a new manager takes control of a football club. He wants to impress, we want to make an impression on him and for a few days it was a question of standing back and watching George Graham. As manager of Millwall, he couldn't have seen Arsenal play a great deal and he wanted to know the strengths of some of the players. This was to become obvious during the early weeks of the season when the boss would often ask the senior players: 'What are the strengths of this opposition?' or 'How do they usually defend at free-kicks?' and he frequently sought my advice over strengths and weaknesses within the club.

The early days are important for the younger players. They are easily influenced and the boss was clearly looking for reactions from them. His message today was that Arsenal have a lot of experienced players but we have not won anything, and we certainly couldn't argue with that. George Graham's determination came through straight away and he said: 'I want to win things as much as you.' It was made clear that we were starting from scratch as a group, that the kids and the senior players were on the same level under the new manager.

Wednesday July 23

The boss asked me today if I was still disappointed about the World Cup and I had to answer yes because the tournament made a deep impression on me, and I had wanted to succeed so badly. It helped, however, being under new management at Arsenal. New faces, fresh ideas help to take your mind off disappointment.

George's assistant is Theo Foley, a man whose reputation I knew but had never met. I am a great believer in judging people at first hand and Foley's early impression on us all is his infectious love of the game and enthusiasm about everything he does. The number two always gets close to the players early on and Theo took great delight in mixing with us in the early days of pre-season training. His Irish sense of humour went down well with the Dublin boys and he got a lot of stick as we compared his warm-ups to those of the previous management team, Don Howe and John Cartwright. It became a standing joke that whenever the England players left to report for international duty we would tell Theo: 'We are going to see Don for some proper warm-ups.'

Theo's preparation for training is totally different from Don's. It is not so rigid, more free and easy and the players soon began to enjoy themselves. Theo admits that he is not the best coach or number two in the world but these are his methods and it is up to us to carry them out. No one has taken liberties with Theo and yet you get the impression that if you cross the danger line he could react. If you want to get Theo annoyed just call him 'Don'. There is however no question that you don't take liberties with George Graham! The chemistry is clearly right between George and Theo and it reminds me a great deal of the relationship that Terry Venables and Allan Harris have formed. Terry is the brains while Allan does a lot of the donkey work. I call the number two the bits and pieces man, he sweeps up behind the boss and does a lot of the liaison work between the players and the management regarding meetings, hotels, and warm-ups and so on. You never see George ordering Theo about and they obviously have a great deal of respect for each other. Even after a few days it seems a great partnership.

Thursday July 24

All the pre-season training was done at our training headquarters at London Colney. We had to be there at ten o'clock, ready to start at 10.15 and the day was in two sessions. We trained throughout the morning until 12.30 and then, after a 45 minute break for rest and drinks (cold juice or hot tea) we started again and went through until about 4.30 pm. Training under Theo and George is as hard as you want to make it. Someone may ask you to run ten miles, but you can work just as hard by playing in a five-a-side game. Since I joined Arsenal from Crystal Palace six years ago the system of players training together has always been the same. Six first team players, three reserves and three apprentices were mixed up together in the early days. This is done to bring continuity and understanding throughout

Opposite: Taking Graham Rix for a ride in the pre-season photo call at Highbury.
(Doug Poole)

the club. So it is interesting that whenever George tries a new idea, a free kick or a training method he makes sure that the entire staff is watching. It means that if a player is picked for any Arsenal side he will not be surprised by the job he is asked to perform. Arsenal sides play the same way and the method is drilled into every player right through the club. Again, this is what Terry Venables did at Palace and the influence Terry has had on George is obvious.

Friday July 25

It didn't take long for the boss to concentrate only on the first team squad. He asked us every day: 'You are good players, why haven't you won anything?' We talked about the way he wanted us to play, ideas were thrown into the air and either forgotten or picked up.

Graham's first priority was clearly the defence. Today he concentrated on us all the time and this was to be a feature of our build-up for the new season. 'The shape of the side has got to be right,' he said and everything was geared to Arsenal not giving goals away. That was his attitude at Millwall and now he was putting his ideas and methods into operation with better players.

My mind went back to our conversation in the wine bar when I accused him of being too defensively minded. I believed that at the time but working with him at close quarters I could see exactly what he wanted to achieve. He wanted Arsenal to play from the back having established a rock on which to build.

Monday July 28

The back five was quickly formed. John Lukic was the automatic choice in goal, with Viv Anderson at right-back, David O'Leary and Tony Adams in the middle and myself at left-back. Tommy Caton desperately wanted to be a first choice central defender and thought he was going to get in when Arsenal surprisingly sold Martin Keown to Aston Villa in May. Keown had come into the side at the end of the previous season and looked a good prospect but there had been stories of him wanting a new improved contract and that went against one of Graham's principles. He had told us all that no one was getting a pay rise until we had proved ourselves to him. Again the message was the same for the kid at the bottom of the club and for me the club captain. Reputations meant nothing.

Keown was not the only player to leave Highbury. Tony Woodcock and Paul Mariner, two vastly experienced England internationals, were on their way. The boss was either trying to reduce the wage bill or had seen something in the kids that he liked better!

I admit I was surprised at the decision to allow Mariner to go. Paul is a great influence on the kids and I believe he could have done a superb job for the youngsters, even if it meant him helping them gain experience in the reserves. When I was a youngster at Palace and played in the reserves I know how I looked to the senior players for guidance.

Tuesday July 29

It is defending every day. Six forwards against the back four with them pushing us back and us playing our way out of trouble. We are determined to make it work and usually we force back to the halfway line. It injected terrific confidence into the defence and paved the way for the understanding that was to develop throughout the season. George kept drumming it into us that he wanted the number of goals conceded cut in half for the new season. And he meant it.

There are new standards being set on and off the pitch. The boss has told Charlie Nicholas and Graham Rix that they can't wear their earrings when on club duty and they have accepted it. He also wants us to wear the same blazers and slacks when travelling around the country as Arsenal Football Club and I am 100 per cent behind that decision. I believe Arsenal should be the best in everything it does and, like England, its players should act as ambassadors.

It is easier for George to introduce these things as a new manager and I now realise how hard it must have been for Don Howe. He was number two under Terry Neill and to suddenly take control and treat senior players in a different way is difficult. If one day you are called Don and mucking about with the players and the next you want to be called boss and have a more aloof attitude, eyebrows are raised.

Wednesday July 30

Training is not all physical and George does not believe in cross-country runs. For the first time as an Arsenal player I am not asked to go jogging around the Hertfordshire countryside. We are doing a lot of straight runs, 'doggies' and 100-metre circuits including 30-metre jogs and 70-metre sprints. The longest we run for is 12 minutes and every time there is a break. We are working hard and the players are enjoying the new routines.

Training is always split into two sections, perhaps ball work in the morning and then more physical stuff after a lunch break of hot tea. The emphasis is always on the defence although there is a lot of attention given to ball skills. The boss clearly wants us to combine resilience with technique. He is encouraging Charlie to do his tricks within the framework of the side.

We formed a big circle today and we each took it in turns to set the pace 40 yards ahead of the rest. Then the player at the back of the group had to keep sprinting to the front. Jog for a minute, then two minutes . . . it went on for ages. The fittest players so far are Stewart Robson, Gus Caesar, Martin Hayes and David O'Leary.

Sunday August 3

Sporting Lisbon 0 Arsenal 0
Our first pre-season friendly, organised after the transfer of one of our old players, Raphael Meade, to Lisbon. I miss it with a slight leg injury; it is not worth taking the risk in matches like this and I didn't even travel with the party.

Tuesday August 5

Arsenal 0 Celtic 2

This was David O'Leary's testimonial, the reward for years of loyal service at Highbury. Celtic are always a favourite opposition for testimonial matches because they bring a good crowd of supporters with them. This game had an extra edge for David because his brother, Pierce, is in the Celtic side.

We played fantastically well in the first half and how we didn't score I will never know. It was 20 per cent of the old Arsenal and 80 per cent of new ideas and fresh ambition. We lost but it doesn't matter. We played some great football and George Graham is delighted. He can clearly see his hard work on the training pitch being transformed onto the pitch.

Sunday August 10

Shamrock Rovers 0 Arsenal 2

Scorers: Davis, Rix

The start of our tour to Southern Ireland. The matches were combined with some hard work; the boss all but took the training ground at Colney with him and the defence again came under scrutiny.

When we arrived in Ireland he warned us that we were going to get damn fit and allowed us to have a few drinks on the first night. He just said go and relax because tomorrow is going to be hard. Footballers don't want to get smashed every night although it is good to be treated like adults and we took advantage. David and Niall Quinn are the local lads and they knew where to take us. In the pub that night I had a £50 bet with a local lad who said that we wouldn't beat Manchester United on the opening day of the new season. It is a pity that I lost his telephone number!

We were still working hard on many training pointers and this was emphasised against Rovers when they caused us a few problems with the long ball over my head for the winger to race onto. Next day it was back to the training ground to eliminate the problem. The back four must know when to drop off or not and George was determined to drill this into us until we performed it like clockwork.

Wednesday August 13

Waterford 1 Arsenal 1

Scorer: Allinson

Our pre-season training seemed to catch up with us tonight and the lads were tired and jaded. The pitch was terrible, very heavy going and we could have lost. The results in these matches are not important but the shape and progress of the side is. We believe we are moving towards the big kick-off in good shape. I recall that West Ham once lost every pre-season match and started the season in superb form, going top of the table after a few weeks. We have nothing to worry about.

Friday August 15

Southend 0 Arsenal 1
Scorer: Allinson

A good match and a good workout. Southend are extremely fit and we responded with another encouraging performance. The boss is pleased, particularly with the performances of some of the younger players. There are clear indications that they are becoming more confident; Martin Hayes came on as substitute and looked especially sharp. The boss loves pace and is certain to have noted Martin's control and acceleration.

4

ON OUR WAY

Monday August 18

The big kick-off is close now and everything is geared to Saturday's visit of Manchester United. You couldn't get a better fixture to start the League season and there is a real buzz around the place. United create massive interest, bring huge support, and with Arsenal having a new manager the headline writers are having a field day.

Our team pattern is set now but we still go over everything time and again. There is a lot of physical work and the first team take on the youth side, the reserves play us and the players are mixed up to appreciate what each one is trying to achieve.

The boss wants a settled first team from the word go. If you look at the really successful sides like Liverpool they have a group of players who rarely move out of the team. That is what the boss wants at Highbury. A determination to be like Liverpool is his motivation.

Saturday August 23

Arsenal 1 Manchester United 0
Scorer: Nicholas
A great result, but a bad game in front of an impressive first-day crowd. Good starts are important to fans and young players, although senior professionals know that a pattern isn't set until a few weeks into the season. Football has a history of pushing clubs high up the First Division after good early-season form and then watching them tumble when things start to settle down. I was happy with the win and yet I knew it meant nothing,

It was a game of few chances. There was a marvellous mood of anticipation before the kick-off and the dressing-room sounded like a boxer's corner as we shouted instructions to each other and the young players in the side like Tony Adams and David Rocastle moved towards the dressing-room door with a mixture of excitement and tension pumping through their veins.

The side was the one that had been taking shape throughout our build-up and we did OK without pulling up any trees. The boss is pleased, although he knows by looking at our past record that this is nothing to get carried away about. So many times in the past we have won well and been a different side the next week.

Above right: Paul Davis shoots for goal in our opening League game against Manchester United.
(Doug Poole)

Below right: Charlie slips the ball past United 'keeper Chris Turner to sew up three points.
(Doug Poole)

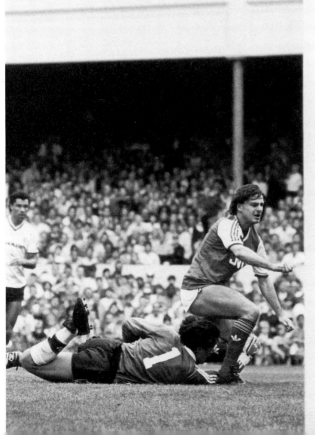

It was a late goal and the crowd were delighted it was Charlie that got it. That should put a few more on the gate for our next game! The boss has just said well done and to expect an inquest into the mistakes on Monday morning.

Monday August 25

Pulling Saturday's performance apart was to become a Monday morning ritual. The boss said that against United there were encouraging signs but we could do a lot better. He did it in a professional way and there was no intention of criticism in his advice. This also was a feature of George Graham. He stamped his personality and authority on the players in his own way; it was done professionally and quietly. It happened before your eyes without you realising how or why. Little things were changed and done as if they were obvious and the kids responded all the time.

As usual, we did more defensive work today with the front six playing against the back four. Hardly a day went by without some form of work with the defenders. He wants to bed down exactly how we are going to play for the rest of the season . . . and beyond. The boss is single-minded and has his rigid plans for the club and his players, you can be certain of that.

He hadn't got me playing in any new style, although perhaps Viv and I were pushed a little more forward. Most full-backs are around the back of the centre-half while we were told to push forward and that applied right the way through the side. The boss wants angles and shape throughout the team, and not to be caught square in any department. The defence is known as the arc at Highbury.

Tuesday August 26

Coventry 2 Arsenal 1
Scorer: Anderson
Our first defeat and yet there were real encouraging signs. The boss is pleased and there is no mood of despondency in the dressing-room after the game. Coventry looked a sound, compact unit and I believe they will surprise a few people this season and have a good time. Cyrille Regis looks as though he wants to play again and I was very impressed with their goalkeeper Steve Ogrizovic, who made some good saves and commands his area well.

Viv got our goal and that didn't surprise me. He is one of the tips I gave to the boss before the season started when he asked me who was good in the air. I told him that I thought Viv was one of the most dangerous players in an opponent's box I had seen. I'm sure this goal will be the first of many for him this season.

Viv is non-stop around the club and his enthusiasm is infectious. The kids love him and his favourite saying before we go through the dressing-room door is 'Clean sheet, clean sheet'. He is great fun in training and tells us all 'Saturday counts'. He is bursting to play and I'm certain he is lined up for one of the best seasons of his career. A fine player – and also the biggest mickey taker in the club. Viv is forever pulling players' legs with jokes and sayings. He is one of the most popular people at Highbury and the boss and Theo really like and respect him.

Thursday August 28

The boss likes players to air their own views and the exchanges can become fierce if we disagree. That is healthy, however, and this day was no different with the players discussing what went wrong against Coventry. To sort out some of the problems, we had a match against the reserves. The youth team players were brought over every time George tried something new. 'Whenever you play I want it done this way,' he shouted and left no one in doubt about his plans for the future.

There is rarely criticism for individuals. It is done as a unit. If I have made a mistake it is corrected in the framework of the team out on the practice pitch. The only time the boss has a go at you individually is if you are making a mistake consistently, and this is usually done in private. I can see so much of Terry Venables in the boss. Perhaps that is a good sign for us because everything Venners touches turns to gold!

Saturday August 30

Liverpool 2 Arsenal 1
Scorer: Adams
The youngsters grew up a bit today and it is already clear that Liverpool, again, are going to be the team the rest of us will have to beat to win anything. Even at this early stage they look just as solid, just as dangerous. We gave Rushy an inch and he pounced with his usual expertise. The boss is disappointed because after all our hard work in pre-season with the defence we have now conceded four goals in two matches. That goes against the grain because he wants us to be the 'mean machine'.

Monday September 1

More defending, more hard work. The back four against six forwards. The boss is determined to get it right and will not be satisfied until we are consistently producing 'clean sheets'.

I am not taking any real notice of other results around the country yet. It is so early in the season and nothing can be predicted. Liverpool and Everton, you can bet, will be there all season. The rest have yet to show their colours.

Tuesday September 2

Arsenal 2 Sheffield Wednesday 0
Scorers: Adams, Quinn.
Our best performance so far and we play some great stuff. Wednesday can be powerful and intimidating but they tried to take us on with football and we overpowered them. In the dressing-room I thought to myself: 'That was a good performance. Could this be the beginning?'

The boss played it down and is clearly trying to keep us on our toes,

Below: Tony Adams takes to the air as John Lukic foils Clive Allen in our 0-0 draw with Spurs at Highbury.
(All-Sport/Michael King)

Saturday September 6

Above right: Tussling with Clive Allen . . .
(All-Sport/Simon Bruty)

Below right: There must be easier ways to earn a living!
(All-Sport/Simon Bruty)

reminding us that we have been through this before, a good performance and then frustration. And yet the team appears to be taking shape and if we can keep clear of injuries it could be a good season for Arsenal. In our first four matches we have kept the same team together and that is another good sign.

Arsenal 0 Spurs 0
I had warned myself about coming down to earth with a bump and what a disappointment this game was. The first derby of the season, the first for new managers George Graham and David Pleat of Tottenham, and yet the match was an anti-climax.

All the players on the pitch seemed to be too tense and there was no real excitement for our biggest crowd of the season so far. Ray Clemence made one great save and that is the nearest we came to a goal. The boss is extremely disappointed and says this is typical Arsenal. We are Jekyll and Hyde and just can't afford to be so inconsistent. 'This is why you haven't won anything,' he says, and we can't disagree.

Sunday September 7

Time to reflect and prepare for the first England match of the season. The England squad meet up later tonight at six o'clock and so Elaine and I take the girls out for lunch and try to have a family day as far as it is possible. Travelling with England has become part and parcel of my life and it is still a great honour to represent my country – though I would have felt happier today had we beaten Tottenham!

Monday September 8

It is good to be with the England players once more. We talk about the World Cup and inside the camp there is a feeling of starting all over again, despite this season being the start of our European Championship campaign. We all agree that the World Cup was a bitter disappointment and that we could have done better.

We trained in the morning and then flew from Luton Airport by charter flight to Gothenburg in Sweden. The pattern of all England trips is very much the same, with Tuesday the concentrated training day and Wednesday match day. It is not so much preparation when you consider the importance of some of these matches. It is no wonder Bobby Robson complains but it is an old problem and throws up a very familiar question: do we play too much football?

Tuesday September 9

The manager launches his latest book and the reception is a nice break from routine. The Under-21 team are in Sweden although they are staying in a different part of the country and play their match today and draw 1–1. I'm pleased to hear that Tony Adams does well and is already being tipped for a long international future.

Wednesday September 10

Sweden 1 England 0
A terrible game, one of the worst pitches I have played on and a bitterly disappointing performance by us. The lads looked tired and the only consolation is that the match was a friendly. Bobby Robson says he learned his lesson when Denmark beat us in the opening match of the 1983–84 season and he has never started a season with a competitive match since. His argument is that he wants us to get a bad result out of our system, and after this we can blame him?

We were certainly not at full strength against a bunch of Swedes who pushed and shoved us into mistakes. Terry Butcher admitted that he had a bad game and I felt really sorry for Kerry Dixon of Chelsea, who played in place of the unavailable Gary Lineker. It was a gamble and one that backfired. Kerry looked a shadow of his old self, wasn't given any service and missed the only chance he had late in the game, although the ball did bobble up at the last moment. Poor Kerry, he really looks under pressure. Our misery was completed when the plane home was delayed and we had a two hour wait at the airport.

Saturday September 13

Sweden's Peter Larson clears from Kerry Dixon on a miserable night for England.
(Bob Thomas)

Luton 0 Arsenal 0

I hate plastic pitches and couldn't tell you five players who enjoy playing on them – and that includes the Luton team. These pitches are just not good for football. In ten years' time we may laugh at grass but for the time being footballers don't like going to Luton and Queen's Park Rangers. Everything is unnatural, you must wear different boots, the bounce of the ball is unpredictable; if it is wet the pitch becomes

slippery and tackling is likely to cause a graze or more serious injury. One thing I will say about Kenilworth Road – it is better than the surface at Queen's Park Rangers' Loftus Road stadium. That is a disgrace and should be dug up.

There is also a lack of atmosphere when matches are played on artificial surfaces. You have to motivate yourself in a different way and in the dressing-room before the game I had my doubts. I wanted to win because we owed Luton something for knocking us out of the FA Cup last season, but it wasn't to be.

Steve Williams came into the side for our first chance of the season because Stewart Robson had picked up a groin strain. In the end we didn't do too badly and got an honourable goalless draw. If we had raised our game slightly we would have won. The defence is definitely coming together, Viv 'Clean Sheet' Anderson is pleased and so are the boss and Theo. It has been a long week and I can't wait to put my feet up with the family at home.

Monday September 15   A clear week and a chance to concentrate on all our faults. We start with more work on the defence and the boss seems pleased with the progress the side is making. If only we can rid ourselves of this inconsistency, we may have a chance of winning a major trophy.

Players don't like weeks with no matches. I know the managers and top brass say we play too many games but ask any professional footballer and he will say straight away that he would rather play games than train. Having said that, the players responded well to a week of hard work.

Saturday September 20   Arsenal 0 Oxford 0

Back we go again. Up one minute, down the next and we can't get it right. We had so much possession, controlled the game and yet failed for the third successive match to get the ball in the net. There is no question that we are getting frustrated because points are slipping through our fingers and it is about time we started to get a pattern to our season.

The boss is under terrible pressure to buy. The newspapers are full of our goalscoring crisis and are demanding that the club buys someone. The boss is quoted as saying that he will only sign a player if the right one comes along and that he will not be bulldozed into a signing.

Niall Quinn, our big, tall centre-forward is the player under most pressure. I hope that the boss doesn't replace him with a new face. I believe Niall is going to be a great player and that the boss would be wasting money on a replacement. I rate Niall, although the pressure does seem to be getting to him. He has so much ability for a tall man and his touch and control is improving all the time. All he needs is confidence. Graham Rix is his close friend in the club and I am sure that he has been helping Niall through this difficult time. All the players rate him and hope that he comes through. Don't buy yet, George!

Monday September 22

The emphasis is on big Niall today. We trained hard and worked at getting more players forward in support of the front players and creating chances. I think the boss has had a word with Niall; I hope it is good news. He is definitely worth sticking with.

The boss is quoted in the papers as saying that he is building a new Arsenal and that it will take two years before he gets the squad together he wants. That makes sense although the man on the terrace is getting frustrated. We need some good results soon.

Tuesday September 23

Arsenal 2 Huddersfield 0
Littlewoods Cup, second round, first leg.
Scorers: Davis, Quinn
We are expected to beat Huddersfield and yet the boss is delighted with our performance. It is his first cup game as Arsenal manager and he says we played really well. This is the kind of match that we have struggled in before and the boss left nothing to chance with detailed reports on their players and how they play. We had a terrible experience against Walsall a couple of seasons ago in this competition and were determined not to let anything like this happen again.

We never got going against Walsall but tonight overpowered Huddersfield with a Liverpool-type display. Liverpool never seem to have hiccups in matches against unfancied opposition and George keeps telling us how he wants to emulate Liverpool. No one knows their secret and all the boss wants is for us to get a little bit of them into our play. I am delighted that Quinny got a goal tonight.

Saturday September 27

Nottingham Forest 1 Arsenal 0
We always play well at Forest, and this was another occasion when the boss asked us, 'You know this lot better than me, how do we play them?' He is learning about the First Division and not afraid to admit it.

We did so much attacking and yet couldn't score and it is now four games ago in the League since we last got a goal. We should have equalised when Graham Rix had a perfectly good goal disallowed. We created chances and deserved to come away with at least a point. The one good sign, even in defeat, is that we have only conceded one goal in our last five matches. 'Clean sheets'.

The match was marred by a nasty injury to Charlie. He collided with their goalkeeper and received a terrible gash across his knee. It was so bad that when Viv arrived on the scene he turned Charlie's head away because the cut was so deep. Charlie was injured right by the Forest goal and their fans started to chant 'Let him die' and it brought a swift

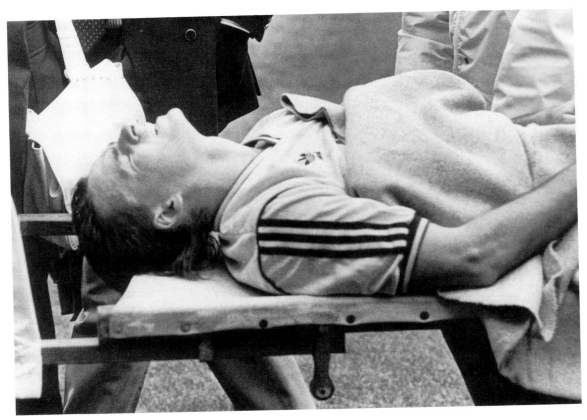

Charlie can't hide the pain as he is stretchered off during our League game at Nottingham Forest.
(Nottingham Evening Post)

reaction from Brian Clough. Clough jumped out of his dugout seat, went berserk and gestured towards his club's fans. He told them to belt up and even spoke to Charlie as he was carried around the pitch on the stretcher. We appreciated it and I am sure Charlie did.

Charlie was taken straight to the hospital to have the cut stitched and we picked him up on the way home after the game. Charlie was in a lot of pain, had nowhere to lie down on the coach and had to sit with his knee almost bent the entire journey. It was very uncomfortable for him and resulted in the club building a bed into the coach. It made sense because Charlie's injury could have been aggravated by sitting up. He looked awful by the time we got home after three hours down the motorway. Charlie's injury brings more pressure on the boss to buy. We are now without goals and our top striker is injured and likely to miss a number of matches.

We go everywhere by coach except Newcastle, and you couldn't get better facilities on board. Television, videos, hot meals, toilets, drinks, waiter service. We sit in the same seats on every trip and there are always two different card schools. Quinn, Allinson, Rix, Lukic and I make up one, and then there is the school I call the noisy lot – Viv, Williams, Davis and Adams. The noise is down to Viv, he never stops.

5

GETTING IT RIGHT

Monday September 29 Hard work right the way through the team. Still concentrating on not conceding goals and working hard on creating more chances. It looks a toss-up between Ian Allison and Perry Groves for the place alongside Niall up front in our next game at Everton on Saturday.

Saturday October 4 Everton 0 Arsenal 1
Scorer: Williams
We have been working hard at set pieces in training, yet this was one not planned. Steve Williams scored direct from a corner and Everton couldn't believe it! The most pleasing aspect of the game was the pressure we soaked up. They pushed us back and we just sat on the edge of our area, allowing John Lukic to see and have space to make saves. We did well on the break and could have scored more and the win has definitely lifted confidence. The last time I played at Goodison we lost 6–1 – my heaviest defeat as an Arsenal player and I was delighted to see the goal go in. The spirit in the dressing-room is very high.

Tuesday October 7 Huddersfield 1 Arsenal 1
Littlewoods Cup, second round, second leg
Scorer: Hayes
For the first time we experience the fierce side of George Graham. He is disgusted with this performance and lets us know it. He says afterwards that the commitment wasn't there and I disagree. We had words and there was a lot of shouting and moaning despite the fact that we had gone through to the next round. It was only the boss's frustration coming out and he said that we showed too many bad habits. 'Good teams wouldn't play like that,' he shouted and it was an evening to forget. But as captain I could not tolerate him saying that the players were not giving commitment. We all desperately wanted to succeed.

 Martin Hayes was the only saving grace in the manager's eyes. Like he did against Southend in our pre-season friendly, Martin came on and played extremely well. He looked confident and scored our goal. It is interesting that a while back Arsenal offered Martin to Huddersfield and we all thought the transfer was going to go through. He is a funny player; on the training pitch he doesn't look as though he has got the ability or confidence to play at the top level but in matches he takes people on and looks the part. This could have been his breakthrough into the side.

Saturday October 11

Arsenal 3 Watford 1
Scorers: Groves, Hayes (penalty), Quinn.
George has worked hard on us since Huddersfield. He didn't like the fact that they created so many chances. It was a ding-dong game and obviously not something that the boss wants us to get involved in.

Before every match the boss likes at least ten minutes when we are sitting down in the dressing-room listening to his pre-match talk. All the little things that players do must be completed by the time he comes in. The boss is not a shouter, although he will let rip at half-time if he doesn't believe we are playing properly. He will not tolerate stupid mistakes or sloppy play.

David O'Leary is very superstitious and has to touch his shoes which are hanging up on the pegs. He always gets changed early and is last out of the dressing-room. Viv usually has a bath, and always goes to the toilet fifteen minutes before the kick-off, while other players have their own warm-up routine in the dressing-room. I have no strict routine: sometimes I warm up in the room, on other occasions I go onto the pitch. I am certainly not superstitious. I am always changed when I take the team sheet into the referee's room and might go out onto the pitch from there. It really does depend how I feel on the day.

We never play well against Watford, they are one of those teams we never seem able to dominate. We struggled again until referee Brian Stevens gave a dodgy penalty and their goalkeeper Tony Coton was sent off for arguing with a linesman. Coton went potty and had to go, although it was a penalty decision that we would have been unhappy with. Watford manager Graham Taylor was bitterly upset and had a go at the referee and linesman. It was all a bit messy until Nigel Callaghan took over in goal and Martin Hayes, who as I expected had been brought into the side, scored to put us 2–1 ahead.

Callaghan did well in goal, almost got to the penalty and made some good saves although he didn't have a chance with Quinny's late header. It is good to score three goals for the first time this season and that will build confidence. The mood in the dressing-room is: 'Let's have a good season.'

Sunday October 12

It is England duty again and I and the rest of the players have to report to the Crest Hotel at High Wycombe by 6pm. Elaine drives me to Wycombe and I won't see her or the kids now until Wednesday night.

Elaine always comes to the England games and then we drive home from Wembley.

The hotel is our usual headquarters for England home matches and there is a different mood in the camp this time because Northern Ireland on Wednesday night are our first opponents in the European Championship.

Monday October 13

Bobby Robson showed us a video of the Sweden defeat and it looks terrible. He notes that from the very first kick-off they put us under pressure. Bad habits. He makes us aware that Northern Ireland always give us a tough time at Wembley and the lads are determined to make a good start in the Championship. It is the biggest tournament after the World Cup and at the back of my mind I know this could be my international swansong. If I am to win something with my country this has got to be it.

Training is at Bisham Abbey and the facilities are superb. The boss likes it and our hotel is OK although there are always a lot of people around and you have to stay in your room if you want peace and quiet. Today is always open day for the Press at training and the players don't really mind that. There is a feeling of being one big family.

Tuesday October 14

The only full day that Bobby Robson and his players have together to really plan for an important game, and that is a crazy situation. But we are used to it now and it doesn't harm confidence.

Some of the players take their cars to Wembley and park them overnight ready to drive home after the game tomorrow.

Wednesday October 15

England 3 Northern Ireland 0
Scorers: Lineker 2, Waddle 1
The climax of a great performance by us was Gary Lineker's second and our third goal. The angle appeared to be too acute and yet he drilled it in superbly. After the match Bobby Robson called Gary the deadliest striker in the world. That was probably emotion speaking and yet if you had a name a striker to score for you in any game it would be Gary. His form is brilliant and his World Cup goals and moving to Barcelona have, in my opinion, made him an even better player. England are very lucky to have him. At the very highest level scoring chances are few and if you have the best on your side it could be the difference between disappointment and success.

It was an important win for us because Northern Ireland have always made it tough. This time they were second best. The manager said it was an excellent performance and he was right. The players are delighted and we went our separate ways after a few drinks certain that this England team would qualify for the Championships in West Germany in two years' time.

Saturday October 18

Newcastle 1 Arsenal 2
Scorers: Anderson, Williams
We could have had six and this was an outstanding performance. We had travelled up to the North East by train, stayed overnight and took the game by storm. We just couldn't believe it when Newcastle went into the lead and it was only a matter of time before we equalised and went on to win the game.

Today there are signs that a real confidence is spreading throughout the team, and Steve Williams has made a big difference. Steve likes the ball all the time and can control the game if the opposition let him. He hustles, stops people playing and his distribution is excellent. If I was against him I would try and prevent him getting the ball and that forces Steve into a corner. But when he is in full flight he is great and today was one of those days.

He does have a few enemies around however and gets himself on players' black lists by moaning and groaning. I don't know how he gets away with it sometimes and he deserves to be in more trouble than Viv with referees. Viv is a moaner on the pitch although he doesn't want to fight and argue like Steve. But that is how Steve plays the game and if it works who am I to complain? We are winning and he is doing a great job.

Monday October 20

We have now gone four matches without defeat and confidence is spreading. The youngsters are expressing themselves more while the experienced professionals want to be involved in a winning season. 'Saturday counts.'

More work today with the back four while skill is developed throughout the side. We are never without balls in practice and that is a good sign. The boss wants to bring out every bit of skill possible within the framework of the team. Good shape, good habits, good results.

Saturday October 25

Arsenal 3 Chelsea 1
Scorers: Hayes 2 (1 penalty), Rocastle.
I followed my usual routine before a home game. I normally sleep in the spare bedroom on a Friday night and take a pill to make sure I go through the night and have a good eight hours. England's doctor Vernon Edwards introduced me to these pills and they really work although some players won't touch them – Paul Davis took one recently and afterwards he said he didn't feel as sharp as usual.

We have to report to the South Herts Golf Club by 11.15am on each Saturday before a home game and I get up around 9.30, have a bowl of cornflakes, some tea and toast and leave home an hour later. There is tea and toast or eggs and beans laid on for us at the golf club but I don't normally eat another thing before kick-off. The facilities at the South Herts are good and Arsenal have used it as a base before home matches for as long as anyone can remember. If you play for Arsenal you are automatically registered as a member.

The boss goes through the opposition on Friday at London Colney and then on Saturday mornings he does it in more detail on a blackboard. We are told everything about all their players, who comes up for corners, who likes to cut inside, who is quick and how we can pressure them in certain situations.

Then we watch football on television, Saint and Greavsie on ITV or Bob Wilson on the BBC and travel to Highbury. I sense today that the players are very confident. It is that good feeling when everyone wants the game to start. As we leave the dressing-room we expect to win.

Chelsea score with a soft free kick and that shakes us up and we hit back in good style to win the game. The boss is pleased, he says that we had a little bit of Forest in us today and a little bit of Liverpool. There are still a few things to iron out although a run is starting. 'Could this be it?' one or two people are asking. It is still too early for me to get excited.

After each home game all the players normally have a couple of beers in the players' lounge and then a majority of us end up in the Orange Tree in Totteridge, a pub that has been an regular Arsenal meeting place over the years. The players are staying a little longer in the lounge at Highbury these days because with success the gates are getting bigger and that means more traffic on the roads. Today's gate was almost 33,000. Ken Friar, our managing director, will be pleased.

After the Orange Tree I normally feel relaxed and happy, especially if we have won. Elaine and I will either visit friends or go out to a restaurant for something to eat. I rarely go home to watch football and don't really enjoy watching myself on the box. I tend to worry about little mistakes that were not obvious during the game.

Monday October 27

Surprise, surprise, more defending today. It has become a joke with the players. David O'Leary and I are pulling Theo Foley's leg about it before every training session. 'Tell you what Theo, isn't it about time we did some more defending?' It only makes the work harder and it is six forwards against the back four again. We don't really mind because we can see the end product out on the pitch – just look at the results and our goals against table!

The dressing-room is great fun at the moment. Monday is always a laugh because of what the papers say. If anyone gets a heavy mention he has his leg pulled, or if anyone of us is quoted he stands to be questioned tongue in cheek by the others. 'You didn't really say this, did you?' 'You don't know how to spell that word, let alone say it.' It is all good fun and only helps to spread team spirit.

Newspapers are not really taken seriously. Some players don't like it if they are criticised, while others take the rough with the smooth. I go along with the latter viewpoint, and believe if you are at the top you have to accept good and bad reports. Everyone is entitled to his opinion. I only react if a reporter or columnist is totally wrong with his facts.

Tuesday October 28

Arsenal 3 Manchester City 1
Littlewoods Cup, third round
Scorers: Rocastle, Davis, Hayes (penalty)
If I win the toss up I always elect to have the ball and kick-off. The opposition skipper then has choice of ends. I toss the coin at Highbury and he calls and the system is reversed for away matches. When we travel I always call heads and the decision is always the same, we always kick off when we can. The boss likes us to start in possession, he believes it gives us psychological advantage and it certainly worked tonight. We pulverised them in the first half.

We kicked towards the North Bank, our favourite end, and it could have been 6–0 at half-time. City didn't know what hit them. For some reason we never seem to play so well attacking the Clock End and tonight was a good example. City came back at us and could even have grabbed an equaliser as we lived dangerously. The boss went mad afterwards.

City had a quick forward called David White and he got behind me from a throw in, something we have been trying to stamp out. The boss had a big go at me, said I didn't play and for the second time this season we disagreed. I had a go back and it was an unsatisfactory way to end a night when we won a cup match. It was the classic example of thinking we had done enough and the boss and Theo let us know in no uncertain terms that we must never make the same mistake again.

Thursday October 30

Trained hard today, our punishment for that second half performance against City. More defending, more talking, more physical work. We are in the mood for Charlton on Saturday.

Saturday November 1

Charlton 0 Arsenal 2
Scorers: Adams, Hayes.
It is pouring with rain all day and we can't believe how many fans are at Selhurst Park, the ground Charlton share with Crystal Palace. The crowd is around 20,000 and half of them are our supporters. It gives us a good feeling as we peer through the rain from the entrance to the pitch.

Charlton give us a scare when Jim Melrose misses a couple of chances but once Tony Adams scores the old feeling starts to pump through us and the result is never in doubt. Martin Hayes scores a great solo second goal to clinch three more points. The feeling now is that we are not going to be beaten easily. It is going to take a good side to stop us in our tracks. A winning feeling is spreading throughout the club. We can't understand how Charlton have done so well so far this season.

Saturday November 8

Arsenal 0 West Ham 0

I like the atmosphere at Highbury before matches. There is a buzz around the place and I enjoy the captaincy and everything that goes with it. The referee normally has some words for me when I go into his room with the team sheet half an hour before kick off; some just say have a good game while others remind me that any rings on fingers must be taped up and in the case of a bomb scare players must come off the pitch. Most referees call players by their christian name on and off the pitch, although we often call them something stronger! I don't really have a favourite official although Keith Hackett would get my vote if I had to select the best.

David Rocastle, Arsenal's Player of the Year, takes the game to West Ham.
(All-Sport/David Cannon)

West Ham were confident and it was a game of few chances. The boss is disappointed because we didn't create more openings. I had a real battle with their winger Mark Ward. He is a tough little character who likes to mix it. All the game he tried to upset me and put me off my stride and I enjoy this kind of opponent. It is a battle of skill and nerve. I much prefer playing against Ward to someone like Franz Carr of Forest who is a sheer speed merchant who could outrun me if their midfield tried to hit long balls over the top of our defence. The boss knows that this could be a weakness and we work hard in training to try and prevent it happening.

Sunday November 9

England week again. We play Yugoslavia on Wednesday and it is a vital international. The lads believe that if we beat them we have a great chance of qualifying for the European Championships. On paper they look our hardest opponents, but the lads are confident and the atmosphere over dinner tonight at the England HQ in Wycombe is good.

I am rooming with Glenn again and we discuss the season so far. We both have new managers and it is interesting to compare the new men with our old bosses. We both believe that Arsenal and Spurs can have good seasons. Spurs have bought big names like Richard Gough while we have stuck with the youngsters. It is going to be an interesting contrast as the season develops.

Monday November 10

Open training for the Press and there are interviews and pictures to be done before we train on our own in the afternoon at Bisham. The England team is like a club these days and it is good to be involved.

Tuesday November 11

We learn all about the Yugoslavs and the boss has details of their strengths and weaknesses. I think we will win.

Wednesday November 12

England 2 Yugoslavia 0
Scorers: Mabbutt, Anderson
You can't stop Viv Anderson this season. He scored again tonight and in the dressing room at the end of the game he was like one of those chatter-box men you wind up. He is so pleased to score goals and there is a friendly full-back rivalry between us about getting them. I remember when he got his first in our 8–0 victory in Turkey before the World Cup. I had already scored for England and he told me before the kick-off he was going to get one. When he did, he turned, pointed at me and danced all the way back to the half-way line.

Viv is so dangerous in the box I don't believe I will catch him now. The Arsenal lads give me so much stick about scoring, or lack of scoring. David O'Leary and I are the only players who haven't found the net this season – I hope he doesn't leave me on my own.

Plug your ears . . . Viv scores England's second against Yugoslavia.
(Bob Thomas)

The Yugoslavs were dangerous early on and we presented them with a couple of chances; Mark Wright had come back into the side and he felt the pace of the game before he settled down. But once Gary Mabbutt had scored with a superb header we were never really in danger. The end of the game was marred by nasty injuries to Glenn and Steve Hodge. They clashed heads and immediately went down in a heap. It looked bad although I didn't realise how deep the cuts were until we got into the dressing room after the game.

Hodgey was carried off but Glenn stayed on with his head smothered in bandages. Chris Waddle told us a funny story about this afterwards. He was on the bench and the boss rushed out to see how badly hurt Glenn was. He had blood streaming from the cut above his eye and it looked impossible for him to continue. Glenn wanted to keep on playing though, and the boss moved back to his seat and kept throwing up his arms and saying: 'He is going back on. Can you believe it? He is going back on. It is incredible. He is going back on.' Chris and the other lads on the bench just looked at each other and laughed. 'What is happening, who is going back on?' But the boss just kept on repeating himself for the rest of the game.

It was a great result for us and we are confident now of going to West Germany in 1988. I had a drink with Glenn after the game although he didn't turn up at the hotel until later because his cut needed five stitches. It is the second face cut he has suffered and he is beginning to look like an old soldier!

Thursday November 13 Reporting back for club training after an England week is always refreshing. They say a change does you good and all the international boys bubbled this morning. The boss has done well to fight off the pressure to sign a new player and here we are in the middle of a good run, without any big signings. The kids have done so well, and I can see them growing in confidence.

The only newcomer this season so far has been Perry Groves, a player the boss picked up from Colchester for £40,000. Viv is the ringleader of the mickey-takers and he gave Perry the full treatment when he first joined. He called him 'baldy' or 'Neil Kinnock' and made him feel welcome in the Anderson style. It is all good humour with no malice.

Groves is very quick, very willing and has performed well so far. If a manager picks up a player like that from the lower divisions and it comes off it gives him confidence. George Graham is his own man, he will sign someone when he knows the time is right, I feel sure about that. He will certainly not panic.

It is strange how players disappear from your life when they are transferred. One day they are part of the set-up and the next they are gone and you only come up against them when you oppose them. Paul Mariner, who left before the season started and is playing for Portsmouth this season, keeps in touch and will always be a friend of the lads.

The leg-pulling and mickey-taking that goes on in the dressing room is never extended to the field of play. You would never get that behaviour during a game. If a player isn't good enough he will not be criticised by other professionals, that is up to the manager. It is not his fault that he isn't up to First Division standard, he has been put there by the club. All the other professionals ask from their team-mates is 100 per cent effort. Footballers can't stand big heads however. If someone thought he was better than he was and began to show off in the dressing-room he wouldn't last ten minutes. He would get slaughtered – Anderson style.

Charlie is a great example of the team spirit at Highbury. In the fans' eyes he is a superstar, but Charlie has never changed from day one; he is just one of the lads. If he is in the side or injured, it is always the same old bubbling Charlie. If anyone turns the hose on Theo it will be Charlie and once he pinched David O'Leary's socks every day for two weeks. Poor David lost 14 pairs and still hasn't got them back to this day!

6

LEADING THE LEAGUE

Saturday November 15 Southampton 0 Arsenal 4
Scorers: Hayes (penalty), Groves, Quinn, Anderson
Believe it or not this was a hard game and we were under the cosh
until their goalkeeper Tim Flowers was injured and had to be carried
off. The boss had a real go at us at half-time because we were getting
caught by the pace of George Lawrence. Once Flowers went off it was
a different story; even Viv scored again! The game would have been
much closer had Flowers not been injured although I still fancy we
would have pinched three points. After the game there were celeb-
rations on the coach because we learned that we had gone top for the
first time.

    The boss was not particularly happy and said that the international
boys looked tired after playing in mid-week. It is difficult to know how
to avoid the sluggish feeling when you are away playing for your
country. We look after ourselves, although I suppose one day to
recover, especially if the England game is away, is not long. Don
always used to say that he didn't like club matches after international
week. We usually got bad results and I accepted the criticism. We were
still delighted to win because Southampton is not one of our happy
grounds – we never seem to do well there.

Tuesday November 18 Arsenal 2 Charlton 0
Littlewoods Cup, fourth round
Scorers: Quinn, Curbishley (own goal)
This was the same as our League meeting four matches ago. We
outfought them and then went on to win the game. It was a no-contest
and in the last few games I had been impressed by the way we have
restricted our opponents to just one or two chances. This is our fourth
clean sheet and all the defensive work on the training pitch is paying
off.

Opposite: Tony Adams,   Tony Adams has impressed us all. As the start of the season it was
one of the brightest stars touch and go whether Tony or Tommy Caton would get the nod or
of the 1986-87 season. partner David O'Leary at the centre of the defence and Tony has
(All-Sport/David Cannon) grabbed his chance well. He is quick, although not as quick as

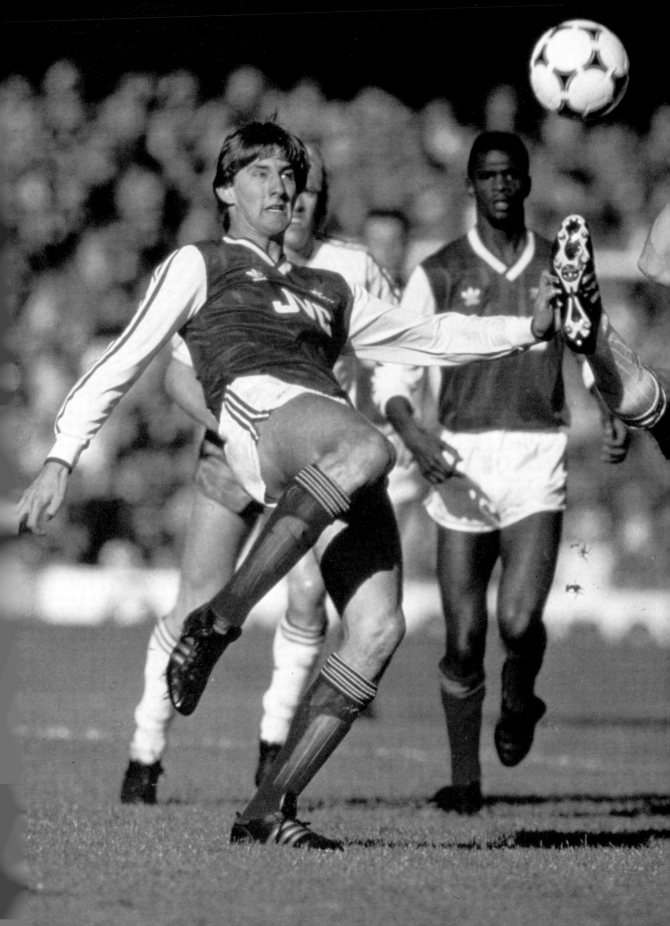

O'Leary, good in the air, a great tackler and very determined. He is learning all the time but is still confident enough to bawl and shout on and off the field and give instructions. He has already skippered the England Under-21 side and he reminds me a lot of Terry Butcher. They say he will be the next Arsenal captain. But not just yet . . . that job is in safe hands.

Thursday November 20   More defending at Colney. We are not complaining because one look at us at the top of the First Division proves that it is working. We have gone ten matches without defeat and confidence is spreading. We are being encouraged to play across the back four like Alan Hansen and Mark Lawrenson of Liverpool and the boss is slowly introducing other aspects of training in the framework of the defensive set-up. We have started to play little games using both feet for ten passes and playing the ball through cones and volleying a certain way . . . it all relates to matches and the opposition and makes training more interesting. It is always a good sign when the lads are hungry to go training. There is a buzz at Colney as soon as we arrive before ten o'clock. The boss must be delighted.

Friday November 21   The boss and Theo love training and joining in. The boss is very skilful and says that if he still had 'his legs' he would be playing with us. When Theo scores a goal in training he goes berserk and often bets us £1 that he will score from an angle or beat John Lukic from a free kick. I can't think how much money he owes us.

     I don't believe footballers have become fitter since I started to play. The game however has certainly become more faster, the ability of most top class players is fantastic. Defenders are quicker, more aware. I'm certain because of that you have to think quicker and the days of one man beating six players to score are long gone. I know Maradona did it to us in the World Cup, but that was an exception. A great goal from the outstanding talent in the world. I can't think of any player in Britain who could score such a goal.

Saturday November 22   Arsenal 3 Manchester City 0
Scorers: Anderson, Adams, Quinn
My first real bust up with the boss. We murdered City, they didn't get a kick and it was a really professional performance. We attacked and defended as a team. But the boss wasn't happy with my performance against the boy he believed gave me a tough time in our recent Littlewoods Cup tie. David White is one of the quickest players I have come across and yet he only caught me twice in the game and nothing came of his speed and possession.

     The boss disagreed and said that my performance was nowhere near my standard and that the lad had given me problems in two matches. We exchanged words and I turned and walked into the shower-room. Nothing else was said and by the time I had finished washing the boss had gone to talk to the Press. I was annoyed because I know when I have not played well and I didn't believe that this was one of those occasions.

Sunday November 23

I love Sundays when we have won. It is a family day and I do all the things I enjoy away from football. Up late, read the papers, play with the kids, go for a pint and home for a nice meal.

I usually get a couple of calls from reporters in the mornings and I have mixed feelings about that. As captain I am happy to comment on relevant situations although often I avoid getting involved. If an incident involves me I want to put the record straight and express my feelings but if one of the other players has become involved during the game on Saturday I believe it is up to him to tell the truth. If I scored a couple of goals however I would be happy for the 'phone to ring all day!

Monday November 24

The boss called me into his office before training to discuss our disagreement on Saturday night. I told him that I thought he went overboard and that I thought I did well in the game. He expressed his views and we cleared the air. I am glad we had a chat because there is nothing worse than letting this kind of thing drag on. It was forgotten by the time we started training.

Tuesday November 25

The boss is still playing down our unbeaten run and the experienced players are happy with that. We have all been through this before and it can end just as quickly as it began. We certainly don't feel like the centre of attention and the boss doesn't want us to get carried away just because we have gone 11 matches without defeat. 'We have won nothing yet' he keeps telling us and the Press. I wonder what his real feelings are?

Saturday November 29

Aston Villa 0 Arsenal 4
Scorers: Keown (own goal), Groves, Hayes, Rocastle
A great day and a great performance. We played so well today the referee, Bob Nixon, stopped me during the second half and said: 'This is great stuff, Kenny.' The lads were terrific and you can imagine the atmosphere in the dressing-room after the game. The whole place was on fire with celebration and anticipation of this being a really outstanding season. It was difficult not to get carried away after the way we played. Mid-way through the second half our fans started to chant 'Boring, boring, Arsenal,' and I thought that was a great touch. For so long we have been labelled a boring side and yet we were really playing top quality attacking football. We have buried the boring image once and for all.

Opposite: Viv shadows
Gary Bannister in our 3-1
win over Queen's Park
Rangers at Highbury.
(Bob Thomas)

We had a lucky break when Martin Keown, our old team-mate, put
through his own goal and it was non-stop Arsenal pressure after that. I
have noticed recently how a goal seems to lift us, the confidence starts
to ooze through the team. Another good sign is that we have not
conceded a goal for six matches.

Before each game the vice-chairman David Dein usually comes into
the dressing-room to wish us all the best, but it is a rule that the room
has to be cleared by 2.30. The half-hour before kick-off is the time for
self motivation and talks from the boss and Theo.

For me, motivation normally starts when I leave home to drive to the
South Herts Golf Club for a home game, or to the pick-up point for the
coach if we are travelling away. I always listen to either Nat King Cole
or Johnny Mathis on my car stereo; slow thoughtful music makes me
unwind and get ready for the battle ahead. I wouldn't dare ask to play
it in the dressing-room, I would get slaughtered by you know who. I
leave the music to the pop fans like Charlie and Viv.

Monday December 1

I know we haven't won anything yet but I have to admit that the
prospects for this season are exciting. People are bursting to say we
could win something and are holding back for obvious reasons.
Training is going to be fun this week – the lads can't wait to play again.

Saturday December 6

Arsenal 3 Queen's Park Rangers 1
Scorer: Hayes 2, Quinn
The boss is disappointed despite another victory. He told us afterwards that had we played a good side we could easily have lost. He
emphasised that our passing was not good enough. What disappointed the lads most was conceding a goal. When Gary Bannister
scored late on in the game for Rangers the back four couldn't believe it.
It was a soft, stupid goal to give away and it was as if we had lost the
match in the dressing-room after the game. There was a great deal of
swearing and cursing. Had it been a fantastic strike we could have
accepted it but to end our 'clean sheets' record like this is
disappointing.

What a great crowd for a League game like this. 34,049 – I wonder
what it was last season. The Arsenal fans are beginning to realise that
this season could be a big one.

Monday December 8

'No more goals' is the message for the defence this morning and we
have been down this road before. It is hard work as the back four take
on six forwards again. The boss certainly means business when he
says you can't win anything without the shape of the back four being
right.

Saturday December 13

Norwich 1 Arsenal 1
Scorer: Hayes (penalty)
The boss told us to battle for the first 20 minutes and we didn't. Norwich could have scored a couple of goals in the first half and how their forward Robert Rosario missed his chances I will never know.

After a few minutes the referee, Trelford Mills of Barnsley, stopped play and called me over to complain about Steve Williams' behaviour. Steve was his usual self, totally involved, wanting the ball, upsetting the opposition and moaning at the referee. He is like it every game but this referee didn't find it funny and he told me to shut the number four up or else. I duly had a word with Steve and that was the last we heard of the problem. Some refs take no notice of Steve, others can't stand it and this was one of them. There was no point in Steve getting booked, we don't need suspensions.

The referee was involved again before half-time however when he rushed over to our dug-out and seemed to talk to Theo. There was something happening behind our box with the Norwich fans and the ref spent a long time talking to Theo. There was more trouble at the start of the second half and play was held up while he raced over to our box again and ordered Theo out. Apparently he had been swearing, the crowd got upset and the referee decided to react. You can imagine the stick Theo took for being banned from the box. 'Thank God you were not in there, the rubbish you shout is a waste of time' was one of the printable verbal attacks he got after the match.

In the first half the boss always sits up in the stand and phones down instructions to Theo and then joins him in the dug-out for the second half. The boss was unhappy at half-time and roasted us for a sloppy, poor performance. Norwich should have been ahead and we accepted his criticism.

We were much improved after the interval and Martin Hayes put us in front from the penalty spot after Quinny had been brought down. I never watch penalties and turned my back again . . . I don't know why it is, perhaps nerves, probably anticpation of winning. I am so keen to do well this season I don't want to witness a penalty miss. I just wait for the roar of the supporters. Martin Hayes has done well to come into the side and take the penalties. He is a very confident lad.

Sunday December 14

We haven't won anything yet but tonight was celebration time at the annual dinner of our sponsors JVC. It is always great fun and tonight was no exception. You know the kind of do – party hats, streamers, a lot to drink and a sore head in the morning. Elaine and I felt old because we sat on a table with three of the youngest members of the team and their girlfriends, David Rocastle, Martin Hayes, and Tony Adams. They are all between 18 and 20 while Elaine and I are 28! So ancient!

There is also a staff table and David Dein set the tone of the evening

Right *The England team which opened our World Cup campaign against Portugal. Back row, l-r: Peter Shilton, Gary Stevens, Mark Hateley, Chris Waddle, Terry Fenwick, Terry Butcher. Front row, l-r: the author, Bryan Robson, Glenn Hoddle, Ray Wilkins, Gary Lineker.*

Below *Venturing into the attack against Portugal. After all our preparation, we failed to create a clear scoring chance.*

Above left *David Rocastle escapes the attention of Arthur Albiston of Manchester United.*
Below left *David O'Leary smoothly gets away from trouble as usual, while I watch on and Tony Adams and Clive Allen appear to be doing press-ups!*

Right *Steve Williams battles for possession with Tony Grealish in our 3-0 win over Manchester City at Highbury.*
Below *Viv Anderson begins our fightback, squeezing the equaliser past Ray Clemence in the second leg at White Hart Lane.*

With Elaine at the annual dinner hosted by club sponsors JVC.
(Doug Poole)

Opposite: Charlie keeps his cool under pressure from Ossie Ardiles in the second leg at Tottenham.

by throwing cotton balls at us across the room. It was soon every man for himself as the balls cascaded in on everyone within throwing distance. It is a night to let your hair down and I certainly did just that. I feel a bit sorry for Elaine because the baby is due at Christmas and she is at the uncomfortable stage.

Paul Daniels provided the cabaret and before he entertained us he sent a few warm-up magicians around the room to liven things up a bit, as if the evening needed warming up! I felt sorry for the guy that came to our table because he couldn't get a trick right. He asked Tommy Caton to 'find the lady' and Tommy found it straight away and this went on for about three tricks before he gave up in embarrassment. It was hilarious to us and the bloke took it well, and to his credit, he beat me with a superb stunt. He asked me to name a card, and I said the eight of spades and he immediately pulled it out of the pack. Then he said 'Name another card' and I thought I would be clever and ask him for a joker and the magician took it out of his top pocket! Paul Daniels was superb, he did every trick possible – like sticking us to chairs – and put on the kind of show that really gets people involved.

My evening didn't finish with the cabaret. When we went in Elaine had said how much she like the potted indoor plants and so, on the way out, guess who decided to take one home? It was a huge plant and when I picked it up you could hardly see me. The branches were everywhere, the water sloshed out all down my suit and the earth covered my shirt front. I managed to get it out on to the pavement where I bumped straight into the boss. 'Had a good night, Ken?' he asked with a big grin on his face. 'Yes thanks boss, just thought I would do a bit of gardening!'

7

HEADLINES – AND HARRY!

Saturday December 20

Perry and David are left holding the babies during our Christmas visit to the Whittington Hospital. I concentrate on the football . . .
(Doug Poole)

Arsenal 3 Luton 0
Scorers: Adams, Quinn, Hayes
The hangovers gone, we played well against a very disappointing Luton team. They were without one or two of their big names and just didn't string enough passes together to worry us. We are heading towards Christmas in the festive spirit. The side is balanced, confident and we have now gone 15 matches unbeaten and eight of those have produced 'clean sheets.' We are surprising a lot of people, ourselves included, and, I should imagine, the boss. Before we kicked a ball this season he said that it would take time to get things right; he probably still believes that, although this run is a marvellous bonus.

Wednesday December 24

It's Christmas time and the day is set aside for the club's Junior Gunners section. A big group of them come to Highbury to watch us train and ask all the players questions. We sign footballs and give them presents and try to make their day as enjoyable as possible.

They all love Charlie. He is their hero and Charlie responds to them superbly. He got most of the questions although all the players were asked different things and the stock question is always to name your best game or worst defeat. I answered my most enjoyable games would have to be during the World Cup while my worst defeat was our 6–1 thrashing at Everton last season.

The kids watched us train and Charlie was up to his tricks. Theo took us for a warm-up around the pitch at Highbury and Charlie decided to cut across the grass and win the race. He didn't realise that it had been watered and his rubber soled shoes slipped halfway across and to the delight of the boys he fell flat on his face and just lay there in the middle of Highbury. The kids laughed until they cried – they have a great relationship with Charlie. I don't know if the management realise how much Charlie means to the fans. It is probably because he is always the same bubbling character. Perhaps if he came in one day on a downer they would notice.

Christmas Day

All Elaine's family are at home with us and that is good because the baby is due and it enables her to have rests and watch our daughters play with other members of the family. I had the normal Christmas Day until we had to report at seven o'clock, a nice turkey lunch, a glass of wine and lots of presents for the family. We are playing Leicester tomorrow and the boss has decided we must stay in a hotel tonight to avoid the obvious temptations of Christmas.

I don't think the lads were too disappointed to stay away on Christmas night. The boss is ultra-professional and discussed it with us all before deciding that it was best if we went to our normal overnight stop, the Noke Hotel.

Friday December 26

Leicester 1 Arsenal 1
Scorer: Hayes
When I left for Leicester Elaine was in pain and it was obvious that the baby was on the way. Had it been our first I would have been worried but she was in good hands and told me that she would be OK and to go ahead and travel. I don't think it played on my mind. There had been no problems with the birth of our two lovely daughters and Leicester is not the other end of the world.

It wasn't a good game. They suffered an injury when Russell Osman limped off and we should have won the match easily. We had 80 per cent of the play and yet only scored once. This is one of the games we will look back on at the end of the season and say 'We should have won that.' I hope it doesn't prove to be costly. I should have scored!

Someone slipped me through on the left of the box and I thumped my shot straight at the goalkeeper. More stick from the lads.

We played in the morning at Filbert Street and by the time the coach got back to Colney and Graham Rix gave me a lift to the hospital it was about 3.30 pm. Elaine was almost in labour and, bingo at 6.10 pm, Harry William entered the world. I have been present at the birth of all my children and I am sure it is impossible to experience anything more emotional and exciting. I think the hospital staff were surprised how much Elaine and I cried. On the way back home I stopped off at the off-licence and bought some champagne for the family to celebrate. I had a few drinks to toast Harry's arrival . . . quite a few!

Saturday December 27

Arsenal 1 Southampton 0
Scorer: Quinn
Arsenal's centenary match and it was good to see all the famous faces from the club's great past. They introduced them to the crowd at half-time and it was vital that we won the game.

Southampton were difficult to play against. Mark Wright played as a spare man, covering all dangers and winning a lot of Niall Quinn's knock downs. We only won it late when Steve Williams shot against the post and Quinny belted home the rebound. Southampton were boring and it was an important test for us to win. We were patient, waited and got the required result.

It is vital that we don't fall into the trap of just knocking long balls at Niall. He is great in the air and dangerous but we need to mix it up a little too. To the boss's credit he knows this and encourages us to use Quinn as the target man in different areas. We call it shadow play. 'Let's mix it up' we keep telling ourselves. 'Don't give the secret away.'

Went home via a couple of pubs to tell all my mates that I had a baby son. We had a party at home with Elaine's family and I let myself go.

Sunday December 28

A bad hangover. I soon forget it however when Elaine and Harry come home. She looked fantastic and the girls wanted to hold and cuddle Harry. I am on a high. I feel dizzy with emotion because things are going so well. Arsenal are top of the League, we are playing great football and I have got a baby son. I am floating and it has been a fantastic year . . . I hope '87 is going to be just as good. I have Sunday and Monday off and the time is spent playing with the girls . . . and looking at Harry.

Tuesday December 30

We really want this unbeaten run to go on and on. If we keep 'clean sheets' for another month, we know what might happen. John Lukic is heavily involved with all the training and he is delighted with clean sheets. We think we are the best organised defence in the country. Someone has called us 'the Mean Machine' in a newspaper and the tag has stuck, we like it.

Wednesday
December 31

We didn't train hard today and went home for a couple of hours before reporting to our Noke HQ to prepare for the match tomorrow against Wimbledon. The kick-off has been switched from 11.15 to the normal 3pm but the boss has still decided to stay away. I am a little disappointed because I would have liked to have seen the New Year in with Elaine and the family although I can understand the reasons for going to the hotel.

It is a quiet small hotel and ideal for us. There are a lot of people about but we keep to ourselves in a small section of the bar. When 1987 arrived I was in bed and I rang Elaine to wish her a Happy New Year before going to sleep and dreaming of all the things I wanted to happen in the next few months . . . winning a trophy . . . qualifying for the finals of the European Championships . . . scoring a goal . . . !

I roomed on my own this time although it is normal to share. When the squad is an odd number I sleep on my own. There are some normal partnerships for room sharing – Charlie and Ian Allinson, Quinny and David O'Leary and John Lukic and Steve Williams.

Thursday January 1

Arsenal 3 Wimbledon 1
Scorers: Nicholas 2, Hayes
The boss knew Wimbledon well. He told us they would try and be physical and for us not to get involved and try and fight them. We had to battle but let our football win the day. There was a lot of pre-match publicity about John Fashanu, a big centre-forward with a tough reputation. Fash is OK and David O'Leary and Tony Adams handled him well. If Fash kicks you, get up, if you kick him, help him up – that was the message.

Charlie was back in the side because Perry is injured. He scored a couple and was involved in the third when their keeper Dave Beasant brought him down in the area. It didn't look like a penalty to me although we were happy to accept it.

I had a couple of drinks at the club and went home. The boss has given us a couple of days off. It will be strange to be off Friday but on Sunday we are playing at Tottenham, the centenary match between the two famous clubs. It is also live on the box and promises to be a great occasion. Tottenham are going well and a lot of people believe that they are the team to end our unbeaten run. It is 18 matches now and we are in no mood to let it go just yet.

Sunday January 4

Spurs 1 Arsenal 2
Scorers: Adams, Davis
I woke up at the Noke feeling strange. There was a dead atmosphere, no television football to watch and I hoped that the other lads wouldn't let it affect them. I didn't have to worry. It was a miserable rainy day but the atmosphere at White Hart Lane is great. It is a big, heavy atmosphere for a big occasion. No motivation needed today.

Two great club servants, David O'Leary and Glenn Hoddle, battle for possession in the 100th Arsenal-Spurs derby.
(Bob Thomas)

We seemed tense before the kick-off and I was slightly worried, but the nerves disappeared as soon as the match began. The pitch was wet, they attacked us from the word go and the tension vanished from our play as we held them at bay. 'Clean sheets'. Tony Adams, as determined as ever, put us in front and when Paul Davis scored from a free kick I thought it was all over. We conceded a bad goal just before half-time and that was the inspiration they needed. They put us under the cosh in the second half and all the defensive work we had done as a team unit helped us again. We defended well and bravely and restricted Tottenham to only a few half chances.

When I first joined Arsenal six years ago I didn't really care too much about these North London derbies. They were just another game to me. Today though it is different and I believe it is very important to beat the old enemy. The fans love it – it keeps them going for months – and so, as I sat in the bath after our famous win, I thought to myself that we had given Arsenal a victory to remember. The 100th match between the two clubs, live on television and Arsenal had won. Great, and I was proud to have been the captain. They can't take these things away from you when you retire.

The boys couldn't wait to get into the players' lounge after the match. Everyone had thought that our run had been going to end and the players were on a high. We took great delight in mixing with the Tottenham players. Spurs were gutted, they knew we deserved to win.

I had a funny exchange with Chris Waddle during the match. He hates playing against me and kept saying 'I hate your face' as he took up wing positions. We are good England team-mates and it was all said in the best possible taste.

Monday January 5

The win has taken a lot out of me. I am tired and spend the day off relaxing with Elaine and Harry. The papers are full of our victory and David Pleat is quoted as saying: 'Who can stop Arsenal?'. That is dangerous talk and before we left White Hart Lane yesterday the boss reminded us that every opponent now will be after our scalp and that it is going to be tough.

Elaine recorded the game for me but I don't like to watch myself play. I have promised myself that I will make a scrapbook of my career and I'm sure Harry will be proud to read it one day.

Tuesday January 6

We are still affected by the Spurs victory. The players are tired and jaded in training and the boss asks us all the time: 'What's wrong lads?'. George and I had a chat and I told him that I thought the youngsters were sluggish and that they were not responding because their minds were still on Tottenham. The boss agreed and we cut short the rest of the morning. A few sprints and training was called to a halt. It was a sensible decision because we are all super fit and there is no need to push the kids if they don't want to at this stage. The boss was calling instructions but some of the minds were not alert enough.

Wednesday January 7

The boss has decided to give us another day off. It is unheard of and yet a good decision. On Monday I got over the emotion of beating Tottenham and now I can enjoy the family and build myself up for the next game. I am sure the other lads feel the same. I went shopping with Elaine and Harry and did simple things all day.

We have sold Stewart Robson to West Ham for £750,000. It is a big fee for a player who has been out injured for a long time. Stewart hasn't played since we drew at Luton on September 13 but he is a good strong midfield player and I am sure he will do a fine job. It is funny because I thought he would be a regular for us throughout this season – strange how quickly things change in football.

Thursday January 8

Theo has been banned from from sitting in the dug-out and fined for his problems at Norwich, and the lads slaughter him in training today. We are back to our best and the tiredness has gone. Theo can't understand why we are so pleased that he has been 'done' by the FA. It is just leg-pulling with you know who leading the jibes.

It is freezing today and the pitches at Colney are too hard to use so we train in the indoor gym at Highbury. We are all amazed because the boss elects to have a five-a-side match! He hates them because he plays with the youngsters and the older side always wins. The boss gets so annoyed with the kids and often calls a halt to the game and reverts to sprints and exercises. Paul Davis consistently gets stick because he insists he should be on the young team. We have to call him back: 'Come on Davo, you've been around for years!'

Friday January 9

Too frozen to go to Colney again. The boss turned up for training at the gym with a pair of gloves on and took stick from everyone. 'If you want to wear gloves, go ahead, they are £2.99 in Marks' was his reply. I bought myself a pair this afternoon, and I will wear them in a game if I feel too cold because if you lose warmth in your hands or your feet the circulation seems to take hours to warm up. I have got bad circulation and I always put a lot of algipan on my hands when the weather is cold. I think I will wear these gloves in the future, although it might be difficult because I take a lot of throw ins. I'm not sure whether the referee will allow me to wear them.

Saturday January 10

Reading 1 Arsenal 3, FA Cup third round
Scorers: Nicholas 2, Hayes (penalty)
Reading's Elm Park ground is frozen solid down the middle, soft on the wings with a hard underneath and it is only just playable for our first FA Cup tie of the season. Last season perhaps we would have been apprehensive about this tie but the lads are confident and I have no fears as we walk over the pitch before the kick-off. The number one Press boys are here looking for an upset but I don't think they will get their wish.

Charlie put us in front and we controlled the game despite Reading equalising. Martin Hayes scored another penalty and, once again, I turned my back. I have to admit I had a bad game. Their right-winger, a lad called Jerry Williams, kept his feet on the pitch, had a good turn of speed and I just couldn't catch him. Their crowd started to call me Fatty and of course this was picked up in the dressing room after the tie. The lads loved it. 'Who are we playing next week, Fatty' etc etc.

Overleaf: Martin Hayes about to be brought down by Danny Thomas in the League game at White Hart Lane. Paul Davis scored from the free kick to give us a memorable win.
(Bob Thomas)

Monday January 12

A bad day for me. Colney was still too frozen to train outside and we went to the gym at Highbury again. Halfway through Elaine rang me to say that my elder brother Peter had suffered a heart attack.

Peter, who is 39, has had a heart attack and a by-pass operation before but this sounded serious because all the family had been asked to go to St Mary's Hospital. When I saw Peter he looked dreadful, as bad as I can remember. His mouth was dry and I had to wet his lips with a cotton bud so he could speak to us.

It is very worrying and I intend to visit him every day. The boss has given us two days off this week because we don't play until Sunday – another live match against Coventry – and this will enable me to help Peter all I can. There's snow and ice everywhere and the girls and I go sledging and skating.

Friday January 16

The boss has been talking about us being feared throughout the country like the old Arsenal side that he played in. They won the double so he must know what he is talking about. We have lost the boring tag for good and now he wants us to be determined, use our strength and earn the right to play exciting football.

I have often been criticised for not kicking more and this really annoys me. You don't have to kick to be a good First Division defender. I don't even like giving away free-kicks! My ideal is a mixture of helping friends and team-mates on the park and creating and scoring goals from my position as captain and left-back. It is as simple as that.

A young lad in a wheelchair was at Highbury to watch training today and the lads made a fuss of him. Poor kid, to see his expression when we said hello was worth a lot.

The doc gave a talk on AIDS today. Arsenal are so professional in everything they do; they decided to make the entire staff aware of the dangers and it made a big impression on the young lads in the club. Dr Crane started by talking about homosexuals and Viv brought the house down by saying 'Don't rule it out!' The doc had a big graph that spelt out the danger of AIDS and his information showed us that all diseases transmitted through sexual intercourse are curable, except AIDS. He told us that it was impossible to catch it from loo seats or showers and baths but for us to be careful if we ever suffered a serious cut and began to lose blood.

Saturday January 17

I don't enjoy not playing on a Saturday. Training just doesn't seem right and I felt weird when John Lukic gave me a lift to the hotel this evening. One funny note today – Charlie filled David O'Leary's pockets with talcum powder!

Sunday January 18

Arsenal 0 Coventry 0

Our first live game on TV at home. It is cold but the undersoil heating has been on for a few days and the pitch is in great condition. As we are top of the table a lot has been made of us and it seems all the country wants to discover just how good Arsenal are. We played badly in the first half and then bombarded Coventry in the second without ever looking likely to break them down. Coventry are much improved this season, they get players behind the ball, defend well and hit you on the break. I fancy them for a run in the FA Cup. We took a lot of stick in the Press for this performance and reckon that they were out of order. The boss was not unhappy and seemed pleased and relaxed after the game.

Before the kick-off I saw Brian Moore, the ITV commentator, and asked him if he would give my brother Peter a mention during the match. Brian is as good as gold over things like this and Peter was delighted when he heard his get well soon message. He was sitting up in hospital watching the game and the response to Brian Moore's message was fantastic. Within a few days he heard from people he hadn't seen for 20 years and was flooded with cards from Arsenal supporters. I am delighted to say that Peter is now recovering well; he needs tests but should be back on his feet before long.

The Football Writers Association had a ladies' night for Kenny Dalglish and we were guests of Reg Drury, the football correspondent of the *News of the World*. Elaine however didn't feel well enough to go so I went by myself. I didn't want to let Reg down.

Brother Peter's heart problem brought out the Sansom family doctor in me; after our match with Coventry I was continually asked about heart complaints and it is no secret that I have my own problem. It is a hereditary complaint and I know that I will need a by-pass operation before the age of fifty. Otherwise, I will almost certainly suffer a heart attack. Peter, my father and other members of my family have been suffering heart trouble for years and I am under no illusions that I face a few problems in the future.

The problems have arisen because the Sansoms have narrow arteries and thick blood. There is nothing wrong with our hearts as such but the blood does not pump as freely as it should. My uncle died of a heart attack when I was a youngster and my father needed a pacemaker fitted after also suffering a heart attack. Peter had a coronary at the age of 32 and had to have a by-pass operation. It is a question of me looking after myself and I avoid all cholesterol, I don't smoke, don't drink heavily, I'm obviously fit and I must avoid putting weight on when I eventually retire.

Showing a clean pair of
heels to Cyrille Regis
during our home game
against Coventry.
(Bob Thomas)

8

TAKING ON TOTTENHAM – AND INJURY

Monday January 19

The Coventry game obviously didn't provide enough goalmouth incident for the television people or the Press. The papers this morning are full of criticism and we can't really understand it. It was a good game to play in and the boss is certainly not unhappy with us. It is a pity that the papers seem to have to criticise.

Tuesday January 20

The papers are full of stories about AIDS in football this morning. It is not surprising because we have already had our chat with the doctor at Highbury.

I have started to put on a bit of weight around my stomach and have been concentrating on doing sit-up exercises. The trouble is the more I do, the worse a little pain in the pit of my stomach gets. It will probably disappear after some treatment and is nothing to worry about. I have been one of the luckiest footballers around and have only had one serious injury in my career, a thigh muscle strain that kept me out for a few weeks. But no broken bones or ligament problems, thank God, and I have never needed an operation. I should be touching wood.

We play Forest tomorrow in the Littlewoods Cup and the lads are very confident. We just don't want our run to stop and, while Forest are a good side at home, we believe they are bad travellers and we have nothing to worry about. There isn't any complacency, yet the confidence is sky high. The boss likes Johnny Metgod and warns us that we must not allow him to dominate the game. He is the kind of player who can suffocate us with his passing, especially if their speedy winger Franz Carr is on song.

Wednesday January 21

Arsenal 2 Nottingham Forest 0
Littlewoods Cup quarter-final.
Scorers: Nicholas, Hayes
As we expected, Forest were disappointing on the night and we were never in danger of not going through to the semi-final. It seems the youngsters in the side just don't have any nerves and the bigger the match, the better they respond. You go into these cup matches with slight apprehension; you know that an off night or one mistake can

dump you out of the cup but once we settled down there was never any doubt in my mind that we would go through.

We didn't allow Metgod the space he likes and Carr, fortunately, never used his explosive pace. Martin Hayes scored again and it is becoming a great habit for him – his confidence is rising with every game and goal.

Thursday January 22

Felt that slight stomach pain again this morning. I know it is nothing but maybe I should get some advice.

The semi-final draw for the Littlewoods Cup was made live on TV-AM and we will play Spurs if they can beat West Ham. You can't get a bigger or more exciting prospect than that and everyone is talking about it. The lads want it to be Spurs, especially as we have already won at White Hart Lane in the League.

Friday January 23

We have now gone 22 matches unbeaten, an incredible achievement for a side so full of inexperienced and young players. The older ones like myself, Viv, and David O'Leary know that runs like this must end one day but the lads won't accept it.

We have a massive test tomorrow at Manchester United. They are not having a great season but now Alex Ferguson has taken over at Old Trafford from the sacked Ron Atkinson and it is obvious they will be going all out in front of a packed passionate crowd. Arsenal haven't got a particularly good record at United and the papers are building the game up. They are all saying that this is the match that will end our record. I have to admit that I am not totally confident that we will win; I think a draw for us would be a great result.

Saturday January 24

Manchester United 2 Arsenal 0

From the first whistle United, and particularly Norman Whiteside, were intimidating. In the opening minutes he caught David O'Leary with a bad tackle and we never recovered from his bullying tactics; we allowed Whiteside to put the frighteners on. Whenever we play United their tactics are the same. Whiteside and Bryan Robson try and hound our midfield and put our back four under pressure. We should have been ready and waiting but instead in the opening 20 minutes allowed ourselves to get upset by Whiteside's tackling. It was late, and yet we should have been more professional in our response.

I must also criticise referee George Tyson from Sunderland. Had he stamped down on Norman in that early period the game wouldn't have been so explosive. United had obviously had a long chat about their tactics and the players must have been behind it because Alex Ferguson had no reason to know anything about United-Arsenal battles of old.

The game exploded when Whiteside went in hard and late on young David Rocastle, Rocky retaliated and the referee sent him off. We were furious because Norman didn't go with him, and the fact that we believed that David didn't deserve to be sent off. He had learned his lesson however; he was softened up by Whiteside and fell for the trap. Rocastle is an aggressive little player, very exciting on the ball and fights like a tiger to win it back. At Old Trafford he discovered that he should have walked away from provocation. That is it easy to say when you are battling in the heat of a pressure game, but it is a fact.

That early onslaught put them on top and they went ahead soon after half-time. As the game developed we desperately tried to protect our unbeaten record and went searching for the equaliser. However our tactics became over-ambitious and we often threw too many men forward, usually leaving David O'Leary alone at the back to look after three United forwards. It was obvious they were going to score again.

There was bitter frustration and anger in the dressing-room. It was not aimed at Whiteside; we were annoyed that we had allowed ourselves to be intimidated. During our unbeaten run we had not allowed anyone to 'boss' us and yet we had been caught by surprise by United, and not fought against it in the correct way. The boss was more concerned about that than losing the record. Runs are there to be ended. It would have been better had United outplayed us instead of steamrollering our unbeaten record.

Rocastle's sending off is annoying because, if we are to challenge for all the top honours, it is important that we keep the squad together right the way through the season. We don't need suspensions cropping up at the end of the winter and robbing us of important people, like David.

It was a sad coach journey home. I reflected on the run and thought about the next few matches. It is important to build again. Let's learn from the lesson. At the back of my mind I am worried that we might suddenly start to forget to do the things we are good at. Bad habits are dangerous things to allow to develop and it is now vital that we bounce straight back against Plymouth in the FA Cup on Saturday.

Sunday January 25   Into Highbury for treatment on my stomach strain. It aches the day after a game and then gets better after rest and treatment. I'm sure it is just a nagging injury that will disappear soon. The last thing I need now is anything more serious, especially with so many important games approaching.

I went to visit brother Peter today and he is feeling much better. We watched Everton play at Forest on television. Everton would have taken over from us at the top of the First Division had they won and after a few minutes Peter said: 'I don't think they are going to score.' He was right and Forest went on to do us a big favour by winning. It softened the blow of losing to United.

Monday January 26

David O'Leary was obviously bitterly upset with Norman Whiteside. One or two papers today are carrying stories from David criticising the United tactics. David is quoted as saying that Norman ran amok and behaved like 'a wild nutter'. He says that he has been misquoted somewhat but I do believe it reflects his feelings. David is not one to lose his head and I have never seen him so annoyed as he was on Saturday.

I went to see Doctor Len Sash today and he hit me with this bombshell. He told me that I need a complete rest from football for two months so that my stomach strain can disappear. 'You must be joking, it is only a strain and I am not in that much pain' I answered and he agreed to let me play on while resting all I could.

Tuesday January 27

Spurs and West Ham must replay their Littlewoods Cup quarter-final. They drew 1–1 at Upton Park and so we must wait for our opponents. Everyone wants it to be Tottenham. If it is Spurs the build-up is sure to be incredible; North London rivals, two new managers in the boss and David Pleat! Spurs should be favourites to get through now, especially as they play West Ham at White Hart Lane.

Thursday January 29

The boss called a meeting today to discuss bookings and the danger of players missing vital matches at the end of the season. He told us that he didn't want us to stop tackling but to try and cut out the silly bookings for dissent or arguing with referees. It is really aimed at Viv and Willow because most of their bookings come from eyeball to eyeball confrontations with referees. Sometimes I don't know how Viv gets away with it and he could easily get sent off for some of the things he says. Steve loves to natter to the opposition and referees. Some referees take it, others don't like it and I am often told to 'get hold' of number four. Had the referees not asked, I think Steve could have been in far more trouble. But I don't think either of them will change. Steve is a fierce competitor, and hates to be cheated out of anything. If he thinks he is right and the other fella is out of order, he will say so.

There is no question that referees have a hard job, especially in the First Division. If I could change one thing I just wish they would get closer to players and try and understand us more. Why not watch games and players more closely when they are not in charge? They could even turn up at training sessions to see how we tackle and react to certain situations. The key must be to use common sense.

It is the inconsistency that upsets players. One week you can swear at a referee, I don't mean have a real go, just something like 'Piss off ref, that was our ball.' Some refs will wave it aside, and tell you to carry on, even swear back, while others will book you. It is upsetting when on Saturday the official smiles and wags a finger and then next week he pulls out his little notebook.

If I kick someone most referees should know that it was either a mistimed tackle or a slip because I am not a physical player and don't believe in giving away free-kicks, let alone going in dangerously. Everyone enjoys tackling and if you took away the challenge from the game it would be a poorer, less entertaining sport. But the vicious tackle needs to be stamped out and that is what referees should be looking at more closely. The assassins are still around – they are getting fewer, but there are still some in the game.

Friday January 30

I am back in training after more treatment on the stomach strain. I have started to take stick from the lads as it seems I only train these days on a Friday. 'This must be a new signing' is the cry as I enter the dressing-room. 'It must be Friday, Kenny is here.'

Saturday January 31

Arsenal 6 Plymouth 1
FA Cup fourth round
Scorers: Anderson (2), Rocastle, Davis, Quinn, Nicholas
Two strange things happened before the game. John Lukic forgot to give Charlie a lift from the golf club. He had to get a taxi and didn't arrive at Highbury until half an hour after us. The boss was OK, he knew it was a genuine reason and there was no question of telling Charlie off. He is good like that; he treats us like adults and only loses his temper when it is absolutely necessary – though you don't take liberties with George Graham.

Also, a lot of my cousins and family were at the game today and so I gave my Mum about 12 tickets for the main stand. She was handing them out before the kick-off when a policeman stopped her and accused Mum of being a ticket tout! It just shows you that they can't tell the difference between a tout and a genuine supporter! Mum wasn't impressed. One cousin has come over to visit from Australia and he is watching his first English football match. It is also the first time Harry has been taken to a game. I hope we can score a few goals.

In the dressing-room before the game there is the usual sweep with Steve, Viv and Charlie betting on three aways and three home wins with a fiver each in the pot. The winner takes all and Viv can't stop talking. He often goes around the room trying to get others to join in the sweep, especially when there are no teams left to choose!

It is vital we bounce back after the United defeat and there is no question of us underestimating Plymouth. Walsall knocked us out of the League Cup a couple of years ago and we know that Plymouth are a good footballing side. In the end it was a 'no contest' and we played some great football on the day. David Rocastle, with a lot to prove, was absolutely brilliant and he tore Plymouth apart. Viv got another two goals; he just can't stop scoring and, of course he was full of himself after the game. He never stops, never.

Monday February 2

It is now taking three days for the stomach injury to settle down. I hope it is nothing worse than a strain and I am at Highbury for treatment while the lads train at London Colney. I broke off from the treatment table to go out and listen to the FA Cup draw on a car radio. Barnsley at home in the fifth round, a brilliant draw and there is a real buzz now that we could be on our way to a Wembley double!

Tonight I went to watch the Spurs and West Ham Littlewoods Cup quarter-final replay and Tottenham scared me to death by winning 5–1. Clive Allen got a hat trick and he is really scoring the goals this season. Though I think I probably took more stick than the West Ham defence – I watched the game in an executive box with Steve Perryman, Martin Chivers and Peter Shreeve and bet them that West Ham would win 2–1! When I got back to my car there were two Spurs fans resting against the bonnet and they asked me if Spurs had scared me tonight. 'Yes,' I said, 'they frightened me.'

Thursday February 5

As I've mentioned earlier, Don Howe said to us on the day he quit that you only realise what a great club Arsenal are when you leave. Being injured I am finding out just how great the club is. When you are fit you hardly ever go to Highbury. You travel to Colney, train and go home, only going to the stadium on match days. When you are injured however you report to Highbury and spend hours there. History seeps through every door, the facilities are fantastic. There were times when I actually enjoyed reporting to Highbury for treatment. I didn't enjoy being injured of course but it was something different, a change to my routine. Bill Graves, the reserve kit manager, is forever telling stories and jokes and he certainly helped.

Perry Groves has been in having treatment for the last few days and he has just been declared fit again. He told me today that I was in line to get the MBE or OBE. We call him Neil Kinnock – do you think he was taking the mickey?

Friday February 6

I haven't been training hard and yet have lost three pounds. I am delighted – it is probably because I have been watching what I eat. You do that when you are not training hard but I was still pleasantly surprised. It gave me a nice boost before the game on Sunday, when we are playing Spurs in the semi-final first leg. It is live on the box and while I don't mind that, I can't say I enjoy playing on Sundays. Money talks though and football needed the TV companies' cash.

Our big problem is that Viv and David Rocastle are suspended and it means that we must obtain a good result from the first leg at home without two of our most consistent players. The right side of our team has been taken away and the boss has decided that Gus Caesar will play at right-back with Perry in David's right-sided midfield role. Perry prefers the left but so does Martin Hayes and it is not worth upsetting the balance of the team too much.

The boss has told Viv and David to play for the reserves tomorrow. Viv doesn't want to but it will give him match practice. I have told him not to swear at the referee!

Saturday February 7

We didn't do a lot of training, just trying out a few ideas for free-kicks. We talked a lot about Spurs however and went over many times how to pressurise them. It is vital that we get a good result to take to White Hart Lane. We stayed the night at our usual overnight hotel, the Noke in St Albans. We are confident that there is no reason why we should not get a couple of goals. I'm looking forward to the game, my injury has cleared as it always does after a few days taking it easy.

Sunday February 8

As you may have guessed, Clive Allen has put Tottenham ahead in the Highbury leg of our Littlewoods Cup semi-final. (Doug Poole)

Arsenal 0 Spurs 1
Littlewoods Cup semi-final first leg.
Our first home defeat of the season, a bitterly disappointing performance. No, an absolute disaster. Deep down I think we are out. Is our season suddenly going to go bang? We just didn't play and it was very much an anti-climax. We didn't pass, we didn't close down in our usual style and the boss was very disappointed after the game. We all were. How could we play so poorly when it really mattered?

What made matters worse was that Clive Allen's winning goal was definitely off-side. At the time I didn't realise and was surprised when David O'Leary and Tony Adams started to rant and rave. Quinny was in there screaming as well and I couldn't understand what they were appealing for. Two days later I watched the video and it was clear that Clive was off-side – perhaps it was our punishment for playing so badly. We just didn't do the things we were good at and after the game I had a go at David O'Leary and Tony Adams for not playing the ball across the back four. All season one of our strengths has been our play out of defence and yet today we just thumped it forward too many times.

In the players' room after the game it was clear that the Tottenham boys thought they were at Wembley. They believed that they had done the hard work and, with a home leg to come, they were through. And who could blame them? An away goal is so vital in these semi-finals.

Monday February 9

Tony Adams is picked for the England squad for next week's match against Spain today and everyone is delighted for him. He is a great young prospect and has been outstanding in our successful season so far. He is quick, tackles like a lion and is learning all the time. It is impossible to say how long he will stay an England player but he has every chance.

Clive Allen is also in for the first time since he played in South America three seasons ago. He had to be selected after the goals he has scored, although it won't guarantee him a place against Spain in Madrid – Gary Lineker and Peter Beardsley have done so well as a partnership.

Tuesday February 10

Trained for the first time since Spurs and the boss worked at every-thing that went wrong, particularly with the defence. We just hadn't played across the back four as we normally do. Clive Allen is a lone striker for Spurs and yet he didn't even get tired. Had he been playing against Liverpool he would have been worn out chasing lost causes.

In the players' room after Sunday's game Chris Waddle said that he couldn't understand our tactics and why David O'Leary just whacked long balls forward all the time. He said that Spurs just didn't worry and left Clive to pick up the pieces. So we spent at least half an hour today just playing the ball across the back. John Lukic was involved all the time, with the full-backs going wide and David and Tony using short balls to us instead of throwing it forward.

I think Sunday taught us a good lesson about Niall. He is great in the air but we mustn't make the mistake of over-using him. We must vary our attacks more with the ball going into feet as well as over the top to Niall's head.

Thursday February 12

The players are still talking about Tottenham and the fact that we could have missed out on Wembley. That is a bad sign.

Friday February 13

Unlucky for some, and Charlie is dropped today for the match against Sheffield Wednesday. It is not announced but Charlie isn't in the squad that travels North. No doubt the papers in the morning will make a lot of it because he is such a superstar with the fans and the media. It looks as though Perry will play instead of Charlie and that is no surprise because the boss loves pace.

Saturday February 14

Sheffield Wednesday 1 Arsenal 1
Scorer: Quinn
How we didn't win this game I will never know. Quinny scored first, then missed another chance as we murdered them. Their goal was a joke. Mark Chamberlain, who is not the best header of a ball in the world, got his head to a cross and it just looped in to the top corner. It was like a slow motion goal and we all just stared at each other in disbelief. If we don't win the League this will be one of the matches we look back on and say: 'We should have got three points at Hillsborough.'

I felt tired today and it is probably because I am not training as I should be. Yes, the injury is beginning to worry me now.

Sunday February 15

It is England time again and I went down to my local pub at lunchtime for a few pints before reporting for England duty at 6pm. Tony Adams looks confident. I hope it goes well for him and, one thing is sure, Viv will give him a few words of encouragement along the way. Tony may not like them but he will get them anyway!

Monday February 16

Glenn Hoddle has admitted in a newspaper article, taken from his forthcoming book, that he has found God and that religion has changed his life. Jasper Carrott made a joke of it on television on Saturday night, saying that Glenn had found God – it must have been one hell of a pass! I told Glenn and he wasn't too pleased, but my England mate is big enough to handle anything and I admire him for going public about something as personal as this. If you believe it there is no reason why you shouldn't say it. Glenn has had to live with big headlines throughout his career. If he doesn't play well, he gets slaughtered, if he does play well they say he is the greatest thing since sliced bread. He will never win and I think he handles it well.

I had my own share of big headlines today when the *Sun* printed an article by me admitting my heart problem and the fact that it runs in my family. Bob Harris, football correspondent of *Today* thought it was a joke and asked me how my heart was. The headlines on the story probably made it look bad but it is serious to me and my family, and there is no question I could have a problem when I'm older.

I trained today and ricked my neck. What with my stomach strain and now this, I feel like a wounded soldier. My neck feels worse than my stomach and I am on antibiotics, not the best way to approach an England international!

This has been a long day because of the travelling and the usual England card school was in operation. It is good to get away with the England lads again. It makes a break from the Arsenal routine – different faces, new stories. But the same old jokes from Viv! Shilts couldn't resist a joke about my heart and asked me if it was OK to go through the airport scanner with my pacemaker!

Tuesday February 17

Saw Terry Venables, my old Palace boss and now in charge at Barcelona, and he pulled my leg about another article I have done in the *Sun* about my old gambling problems. In the piece I described Venners as 'Porky' and he had a right go and reminded me how he used to have to pinch my stomach to tell me I was putting on weight.

Clive Allen and I visited the Real Madrid trophy room at the Bernabeu Stadium and I have never seen anything like it, rows and rows of trophies, cups and awards. The trophy room is twice as long as my garden. Clive was impressed, and so was I when he told me that he had got 12 hat tricks in his career. That is more than my career total of goals! I do love scoring.

Trained and my neck is still worrying me – more so than my stomach.

Wednesday February 18

Spain 2 England 4
Scorer: Lineker 4
A fantastic performance by us and yet in the first 20 minutes I just couldn't get going. I really struggled and it must be this damn stomach problem. Once I am warmed up there is no problem but it is beginning to worry me now. I can't go on like this needing time to settle into a game.

We are not talking about unimportant games, we are talking England internationals and vital Arsenal matches. Why this season? I am so close to winning something big for the first time and I have to get a bloody injury. All these things flashed through my mind as we did battle with Spain in those early minutes. Should I go and see a specialist? I shouldn't be thinking these things during a game. I must talk to the boss. Is it getting worse? Do I need a rest? Do I need an operation? People are beginning to ask me what's the problem . . . hell, Spain have scored!

I don't know what came over Spain from the moment they took the lead. They seemed to think they had the game won. We just grew in confidence and steamrollered them. Gary Lineker scored four goals and you couldn't have written a better script for him: against Spain where he now plays with Barcelona and in front of the fans who watch

him every week. Gary is a fantastic finisher, one of the best in the world. Some people are saying that he is the best but that is difficult to judge. Gary is top class, there is no doubt about that, but there are some wonderful strikers around the world.

The dressing-room is an exciting place to be. It is very difficult to describe a winning feeling, especially when you have come from a goal down and played so well. It was a quality performance and I'm sure we have made a lot of our critics sit up and take notice. It could have been more and Gary even missed a fifth, going through on his own and shooting wide.

Opposite: Tony Adams wins his first England cap in Madrid.
(Bob Thomas)

Above: Gary Lineker rounds off an unforgettable performance with his fourth goal against Spain.
(Bob Thomas)

Thursday February 19   We got home at 4am. I slept in until two in the afternoon and then one foot on the ground sent the alarm bells ringing through my head. My stomach is very sore, as painful as it has been.

The boss welcomed the international players back with the usual message: 'Well done but it is back to work now!' The boss clearly has the same reservations as Don Howe had about preparing for a game after a midweek international.

Friday February 20   I am really worried about my injury. I went in this morning determined to tell the boss that I needed a rest and then I just couldn't bring myself to do it. One look at our position in the cups and the League makes me determined to keep going. Who can blame me?

I am now on anti-inflammatory tablets and I would do anything to get it sorted out. It is affecting my performance and yet I am trying desperately to keep it from the media and the fans. I really have to work on myself to get warmed up for matches – hot baths, self motivation, exercises. It is not right and I am really frustrated about it.

Theo took a lot of stick again today. Viv and I told him how good Don's warm-ups had been in Spain and why didn't he come along next time to get some tips. We have started to call him Don and that shows just how good the team spirit is. You can call Theo anything and he bounces back with a quip of his own, but you don't call the boss names. There is a different respect and the longer the season goes on the more I realise what a good team they are.

Saturday February 21   Arsenal 2 Barnsley 0
Scorers: Hayes (penalty), Nicholas
Not a great game although an efficient performance by us. The boss was pleased because I know he had been worried about the international players not being able to perform to the best of their ability. I felt tired, so did one or two of the others who had been away. But we got through and are in the next round of the FA Cup.

Martin Hayes scored another penalty (I turned my back again) and Charlie came on as substitute to score a great goal. Martin has now got 17 goals this season and that is a remarkable record for someone who definitely wasn't a first choice at the start and it is significant how confidence boosts your performances. Martin is playing as if he believes he is going to score every time he plays and it wouldn't surprise me if he gets way over 20 by the time we finish.

England duty means there are long weeks and yet there is absolutely nothing anyone can do about it. They say that in England we play too much football and the way I feel today I would have to agree.

Monday February 23   The FA Cup quarter-final draw pairs us with Watford or Walsall at home, another great boost for everyone. All the lads hope that Walsall beat Watford in their replay at Vicarage Road tomorrow night. I'm not so sure because I remember what the Third Division side did to us in the League Cup a couple of years ago. It was a day of more treatment for me and I spent hours at Highbury, talking about football and hoping that the strain would ease.

Tuesday February 24

None of the boys are keen but the boss wants us to go to Watford tonight. We play an important First Division League match at Oxford tomorrow and they would rather go home and get an early night. The boss insists however and so we all meet at Colney and troop off to Vicarage Road. It was certainly an entertaining game and when Walsall scored all the lad jumped into the air in delight, much to the annoyance of the Watford fans sitting close to us. When it was 1–1 we decided to sneak off to miss the traffic and go home to bed.

When I got back I switched on the teletext and couldn't believe it when it said that the game was in extra time at 3–3. I decided to get up a bit earlier in the morning and watch the highlights on video – at least I will be able to answer any questions about the game if the boss starts talking about Walsall! It made sense to leave Vicarage Road early because had we waited until the end and then still travelled home it would have been at least 12.30 before any of us got to bed.

Wednesday February 25

Oxford 0 Arsenal 0

Theo got more stick because we arrived in Oxford too early and the lads were unhappy with the arrangements. Then there was a long wait for the pre-match meal and Theo was public enemy number one. A plot was set to get our own back and Theo fell right into the trap in the dressing-room.

At Oxford there is a trough of water you have to step through before going into the shower area. It is quite a dark area and unless you know that it is there you are likely to step right into it. Tony Adams walked through it with his suit on as soon as we entered the dressing-room and Viv quickly laid down the plans to catch Theo.

Viv was to go into the shower room and call Theo through because he needed some help. In came Theo, Viv called out and in he went, right up to his knees in water. The lads couldn't believe it and the dressing-room rocked with laughter as Theo hopped about cursing and swearing. It just shows you the spirit between the players and the management, especially before a match that could see us back to the top of the First Division.

I have never really had happy memories of playing at Oxford. A couple of years ago they knocked us out of the Cup when Pat Jennings dropped a long shot over his head and in the final game of last season we were beaten in a match that saw Oxford survive and Ipswich go down. Those end-of-season matches when there is nothing in it for you but a lot at stake for other teams are difficult to play in. It is almost impossible to motivate yourself because you have nothing to play for.

We faced our good friend and old colleague Tommy Caton for the first time tonight and he played well. It wasn't a particularly good game but Tommy was obviously geed up and defended well against Niall. We did not create many chances, and the most controversial moment in the game came when Perry Groves went down injured after being tackled in the area. It was an obvious penalty but referee Howard King didn't give it and then waved play on as Perry lay on the ground. Perry didn't move and yet the referee refused to stop play and he got a lot of stick from the boss and the players before he finally allowed Gary Lewin on. Once I even tried to boot the ball out of play and missed! Gary gave King some more stick and told him that Perry had to go off. I don't believe the referee knew how serious it was and yet he was wrong not to stop the game. He should have called a halt and had a drop ball on the halfway line. After the game he apologised to the boss and Perry who had his leg bandaged up with a ligament injury. I am not one to criticise referees because as I have said before, they have a difficult job. This time however he was definitely in the wrong.

When we play in London or on the outskirts of the capital we never have a hot meal on the return coach journey. There just isn't time to get anything going and on this journey the boys decided it was a night for fish and chips. They all started singing 'Fish and chips, fish and chips, fish and chips' and, to his credit, the boss did well by stopping the coach and going into a local chippie and buying all the team and staff a meal. It was a great sight to see, the Arsenal manager coming out of a little corner shop carrying bags and bags of steaming fish and chips. How the mighty live! George was a bit upset when the man serving the food asked him: 'Are you going to win anything this year then George?' He should complain, the money he took tonight!

Thursday February 26   Rixy had to ring Paul Davis today and came rushing back into the dressing-room with news of the most incredible answering message you have ever heard. 'It is fantastic' Graham told us. It goes something like this: 'Hello there, I'm out and about at the moment, but I'm popping in from time to time. Why don't you leave a message? Go on, give it a try.' Rixy said we just wouldn't believe it and so all the team rushed out to the nearest 'phone box and fed in 50p pieces, just to listen and leave their own message.

Paul is a strange character and seems to open himself up to such ridicule. It is fantastic how he takes the stick and comes up smiling – all credit to him in my book. He once told us a story about how he came out of his flat and discovered to his horror that one of his car wheels had been stolen. He rushed back in to 'phone the police and by the time he returned to his car, another wheel had gone!

Paul is just one of a number of coloured players on the Arsenal staff and this is a great opportunity for me to say that there is absolutely no prejudice in the Arsenal team. All the lads get on well together and young coloured players like Michael Thomas and Gus Caesar, who have just arrived in the squad, are all accepted as one of us. You hear of things going on in football but I can honestly say that I have never known any problems at Highbury.

Saturday February 28   All our thoughts today are switched back to Tottenham. We play them tomorrow at White Hart Lane in the second leg of our Littlewoods Cup semi-final. It is another live TV game and the pressure is right on us at 1–0 down.

We don't train hard but practise free-kicks and set pieces and Michael Thomas is told that he must do a marking job on Glenn Hoddle. It doesn't mean that he has got to follow Glenn all over the pitch; just to mark him tight in midfield and prevent Glenn using those great long passes. Hod is the best passer of a ball in English football and the last thing you want him to have is the space and time to carve you open.

Sunday March 1   Spurs 1 Arsenal 2, Littlewoods Cup semi-final second leg
Scorers: Anderson, Quinn.
One of our great performances of the season. It was raining, the atmosphere at White Hart Lane was electric and Arsenal proved today that they are a team to be reckoned with again. I was proud of the players; it was a display of great character and strength.

We breakfasted at the Noke to Sunday paper headlines of Arsenal going out of the cup and there is no question that motivated us to prove the critics wrong. The boss is angry about the media. He didn't say anything but I could sense his mood. His message when we went out was to be patient. We know we have to score and yet it is vital that we don't panic, especially if Spurs get another goal.

That is exactly what they did when Clive struck again. It seems he can't stop scoring, especially against us. A few heads went down for a couple of minutes and we were low in the dressing-room at half-time. We won here in the League and yet how many teams win twice in succession at White Hart Lane! Then something happened that transformed the match and turned our sullen mood into one of determination. Spurs announced on their public address system how their fans should apply for tickets for the final and the message boomed into our dressing-room. Then they switched on their old FA Cup final song 'Spurs are on their way to Wembley,' and that took the lads' determination over the top.

This is difficult to describe because it is a feeling that rarely happens to you. You get a goosepimply feeling and you know that you are not going to lose the game. The young faces in the team suddenly wanted to get out for the second half and it was obvious to me as we trotted out that Arsenal were not going out of the competition. Our football was

far more controlled and we began to create chances and pin Spurs in their own half. Viv got the first and when Quinny drove in the second at the far post we were buzzing. The rain came down and yet it was Spurs who looked in trouble as we went for the killer. The fact that it didn't arrive didn't really matter, nor was our confidence dented when the boss lost the toss up for a replay venue with David Pleat. We have to come back to White Hart Lane on Wednesday and we are looking forward to it!

I will never forget that second half performance. It was one of the highlights of the season for me. Arsenal were out of the cup, Clive should even have scored another goal, and yet something lifted us and told us that we were not going to be beaten. One of the oldest sayings in football is that your name is on the cup; perhaps for Arsenal it really is.

Spurs were pleased to have won the toss and yet I could sense from their players when we met again after the game that they were worried. They were too quiet. I remember getting into bed that night and looking back over the game. I went to sleep dreaming of Wembley.

Monday March 2

A day off and I enjoyed reading the match reports. Suddenly Arsenal are a good side again!

Tuesday March 3

I didn't train because my injury is still sore and I refuse to drop out of any matches. There was not a great deal more to say about Spurs and the lads only practised a few more free kicks. It was back to the Noke Hotel and the boss was keen to keep the same routine. Good habits, good omens, good luck!

Wednesday March 4

Spurs 1 Arsenal 2
Littlewoods Cup semi-final, replay
Scorers: Allinson, Rocastle
For some reason something inside me made me go and buy some champagne on the way to White Hart Lane. I popped into an off-licence for two magnums of the best bubbly they sold. I don't know quite why I did it, a little voice inside me said that I was going to get Wembley for my first cup final. It is impossible to explain those feelings. It is a mixture of fate and hope.

The question is of course, can Arsenal do it again? For the third time this season we must win at White Hart Lane, the home of our great rivals. It is a lot to ask from such a young side and yet we all know it is possible. We spoke about the Spurs faces at the end of Sunday's game, the question marks in their eyes. We hoped that Tottenham would once again play their Wembley song and we prayed that we would get the breaks.

Was it our turn to take the lead and stay in front? Surely we couldn't come back from the dead a third time. Once again, however we had to pick ourselves off the floor. It was Clive who did the damage again,

Opposite: Steady on lads! Michael Thomas and Gary Stevens in the heat of battle at White Hart Lane. (Bob Thomas)

pouncing on a low punch out from John Lukic and drilling in the goal, his third of this amazing semi-final. As the noise erupted behind our goal we all looked at Luky. 'Come on John' I thought. 'This isn't the time to have an off night.'

I thought then that we were out and, amazingly, I got some inspiration from referee Joe Worrall from Warrington. As I trudged back into position he said: 'Come on Ken, you can still do this.' At first I thought it was one of my team-mates and was stunned when I discovered it was the ref. There was nothing sinister or underhand about his encouragement, I'm sure he just wanted the game to be a cracker. Like the crowd, he didn't want the excitement and the match to end. Nor did we and we had to get a goal to drag ourselves level again.

Every picture tells a story. Ian Allinson has just equalised for us in the semi-final replay at Spurs. Danny Thomas just can't believe it.
(Doug Poole)

I shouted at the referee that if he was on our side to give us a penalty, or at least a free kick on the edge of the area! It was desperation time and I don't think I have ever been so relieved when we equalised in the 82nd minute. The goal seemed to happen so quickly, to come from nothing. Ian Allinson, our substitute, ran at Danny Thomas and didn't seem to be in a dangerous situation. But Ian is always very positive and somehow worked himself into a shooting position. He seemed to completely miss his first shot and then mishit the second only for it to role slowly past Ray Clemence inside the near post. The goal was in front of our fans and all I could see was a mass of red and white and the Arsenal boys jumping about in a mixture of celebration and relief.

I knew then that we were going to do it. The Tottenham players 'went' in that split second. They were asking themselves the question: 'Not a third time,' and I noticed Chris Waddle with his head on his chest. I began to shout anything at the top of my voice to keep the lads going. This was the time to go for the kill although I fully expected the match to go into extra-time. I would have been happy with that, we were strong now while Spurs looked tired and ready for the worst.

And then, perhaps one of the greatest moments of my career. The goal that took me to my first cup final. A cross from the left and there was Rocky darting in to score with his left foot. An injury-time winner. Excitement, sheer excitement. I didn't know what to do. I screamed at the ref to ask how long to go and thought that he said three minutes. Team-mates were relaying messages from the bench but no one was taking any notice. I didn't really hear the noise from the crowd as all I could think of was Wembley and the referee's final whistle.

There was no pain in any way from my stomach problem. There was pure adrenalin pumping through my body, I felt I could run for ever and jump as high as a house. Spurs sent over a free kick and I headed it clear and quickly asked the ref how long there was to go. When he said 'three minutes' I couldn't believe it. It seemed a lifetime before I heard that final whistle and Arsenal players, fans and officials erupted as one. It really is impossible to relate how I felt in words. I ran 50 yards to jump on Rocastle's back and here are the boss and Steve Williams, in their suits and not caring about the mud clinging to their shoes. The smiles were as big as melons and for once Viv couldn't get a word in edgeways.

I have to admit that I have never experienced such excitement before, it was fantastic. In the dressing-room two crates of champagne went in minutes and the lads took great delight in singing 'Spurs are on their way to Wembley' at the top of their voices. We couldn't wait to get to the players' room and, surprise, surprise, it was like a morgue. We soon changed that and, without boasting, we enjoyed ourselves. Spurs were just so sick that in the end I had to feel sorry for them, especially Clive Allen who had scored three goals in a cup semi-final and still not managed to get to Wembley. It was gone midnight before we got on our coach, opened more champagne and found a little pub that stayed open until two in the morning just for the Arsenal party.

It was one very happy and proud man who slipped into bed that night. Wembley, a cup final, my first major honour perhaps. I didn't sleep for ages as I relived the goals and the moments of a game that I will remember for the rest of my life. I couldn't wait to talk to Elaine about it the next morning and I only wish that she had been at White Hart Lane to share my enjoyment. But I don't let her go to big away matches any more. She gets so involved and the last thing I need is some big home supporter realising who she is, especially at Tottenham.

9

FEELING THE STRAIN

Thursday March 5	I went out to buy all the papers just to prove it isn't a dream. There is the headline: 'Arsenal at Wembley' and I have tucked all the papers in my file that I have promised myself one day to turn into a scrapbook. I don't have much time to dwell on the papers because I am due in Birmingham for a TV chat show hosted by Pamela Armstrong, the former *News at Ten* newscaster who now works for the BBC. They want me to go on and talk about my heart problems, and gambling, and the fact that we have just reached Wembley is an extra bonus.
	I agreed to appear before the semi-final and I hadn't banked on a sore head, or the drive to Birmingham. But a couple of glasses of wine in the hospitality lounge before we go on puts that right and I enjoyed the company and the programme. It wasn't a big audience but enough to get the butterflies going and the nerves tingling. I hope I am not going to feel like this at Wembley.
	There is an interesting guy on the show who turns out to be an astrologer and he soon starts discussing my past and plotting my future. He told me that I am lucky with injuries but that I suffer a rare problem with my shoulder. That caught me by surprise because hardly anyone knows that from time to time I get a sharp pain in my shoulder that no one can explain. 'How do you know that?' I said, staggered by his accuracy and he just smiled. He didn't tell me anything about my stomach so maybe that is a good sign. He also says that April 5, the date of the Littlewoods Cup Final, is a lucky day for me!
	Terry Marsh, the boxer who won the world light welterweight title last night, linked up on the show from London and we had a chat live on the air. I enjoyed the experience, it was something different and a good way to spend a day off.
Friday March 6	Bad news. Paul Davis (injured by a bad tackle from Clive Allen on Wednesday night) is out of tomorrow's game at Chelsea. With Steve Williams still out it means that Michael Thomas and Gus Caesar have got to play in midfield. Charlie is also out and it is going to be a tough game. The lads are confident, after Spurs we believe we can beat anyone. I don't train, except for a few warm-up exercises, because of

the stomach. There is no question of me dropping out however as we are down to our bare squad with all these injuries.

Saturday March 7

Chelsea 1 Arsenal 0

We got caught early and never recovered. In fact it turned out to be one of our worst performances so far. Too many mistakes from too many people and the cup has obviously taken a lot out of us. That is why the boss can't say too much, there is no way he can slag a bunch of youngsters who have just got the club to Wembley.

The Chelsea youngster Colin West took his goal early after a mistake by David O'Leary and showed tremendous pace to get his shot in. Had he not scored then I believe we would have won the game and David Rocastle almost took Chelsea on single-handed at times.

Big David and Tony were disappointing at the back today and West's pace worried them all afternoon. Tony was booked for bringing him down when he accelerated away again. I had a go in the dressing-room afterwards about forgetting our hard work of the season about playing across the back four. I said to the boss: 'We are not Liverpool but we have got to start playing like them.' There was no confidence in the side today and we must not fall into the trap of relaxing just because we have achieved something.

Sunday March 8

There is something in the papers today about me going to Chelsea in a swap deal for Kerry Dixon. I know nothing about it and I think this stems from a summer story when the boss is reported to have asked about Kerry and I know that the Chelsea manager John Hollins said that he would like me. It never came to anything and I certainly don't want to leave Highbury.

Monday March 9

A very busy and important week for us. We must beat Liverpool at Highbury tomorrow night to stay in the Championship race and then we take on Watford at home in the FA Cup quarter-final. It really is amazing how many important matches top class footballers have to pack into a season. I am in a lot of pain from my stomach but have to blank it out because of the number of important matches coming up. It is not bad enough to prevent me playing but it is affecting my performance, there is no question about that.

There was a headline in one of the papers today that worries me slightly. Watford manager Graham Taylor has asked the FA to switch the referee on Saturday because it was the same man, Brian Stevens of Gloucester, who sent off Watford goalkeeper Tony Coton in our League match. Taylor believes that it could put pressure on the situation. The boss mentioned it in passing and I know that Steve Williams is unhappy.

The boss called a meeting to talk about Liverpool and the Championship. He says that we can't afford to lose to them if we are to stay in the race. He loves Liverpool and the way they play and tells us to be patient, wait and not to lose sight of the good habits we have formed. The message is clear, forget the cup final and concentrate on the League.

Tuesday March 10

Arsenal 0 Liverpool 1
We just bottled it. We gave them too much respect in the first half, were too frightened of them. In short, I don't think we are good enough. The boss is furious at half-time, and who can blame him? We gave away a bad goal to Rushy. Perry Groves, who is not good at defending, was supposed to pick up Rushy from a corner and made the mistake of relinquishing his post too early. Paul Walsh headed the ball back in and Ian turned on a sixpence to drive it in.

That is the fourth game in succession in which we have conceded a goal and it goes against the grain, especially after the hard work we have put in. It was one of those games when I felt we would never score, even when Quinny had a shot that bounced along the line after hitting the inside of a post.

Surprisingly, the boss is not too disappointed. He has said all along that we are not good enough to win the League and I have to agree with him. We are short of experience and cover and the pressure on the young lads coming into the side is incredible.

Wednesday March 11

We all visited Bond Street and the menswear shop of Herbie Frog. He is a big sports fan and promised all the lads a suit if we got to Wembley. The boss and Theo came too and it must have cost Herbie a few bob. There are seventeen of us in the squad and suits don't come cheap, especially in Bond Street!

Thursday March 12

I missed training again with this damn injury. I don't know what it is, or how I am going to get rid of it.

Friday March 13

We have lost our last two games and the lads are nervous about tomorrow. Watford are difficult opposition and they can be very unpredictable. They can also put you under a lot of pressure and I am slightly worried about conceding goals. The Football Association have turned down Watford's request for the referee to be changed and I don't think anything of the situation regarding Brian Stevens. I don't anticipate any problems.

I haven't trained today and it looks as though that is going to be the pattern for the rest of the season. If we were not so involved I would stop for a rest in an effort to clear it up. The boss is relaxed and confident that we will beat Watford.

Saturday March 14

Arsenal 1 Watford 3
FA Cup quarter-final

Scorer: Allinson

We scored first through Ian and yet I was never comfortable that we were going to win. Against Spurs in the Littlewoods semi-final Clive Allen had turned to me during the last game and said that our name was on the trophy. Now I felt equally sure we would lose, especially when Luther Blissett equalised.

The goal was down to me and it is a direct result of my injury. Watford had obviously instructed David Bardsley to use his pace against mine and I was struggling, there is no question about that. If he knocked it past me and sprinted my usual legs were not there. I went for a tackle, the ball bobbled and he got away down the right and crossed for Luther to score first time. The memory of Walsall flashed in front of my mind and I couldn't help remembering how Watford had come back from the dead against the Third Division side. Perhaps this is going to be their year.

The boss obviously doesn't realise how badly I am injured. When you are a full-back you rely on pace but when you are worried about getting to things it plays on your mind. At half-time I have to try and hide my own concern and help lift us because there are clear signs that Watford are getting back into the game. My injury is sore and I am trying to think about Watford and yet I can't help worrying that I will miss the rest of the season. I need a rest, there is no doubt about it.

My fears exploded again when Bardsley nipped past me a second time, crossed and John Barnes headed Watford in front. Perhaps John Lukic should have got to the centre and yet I knew he should never have been allowed to get into a position to cause us problems. We start to put Watford under a lot of pressure without ever looking like scoring and then comes the incident that is to dominate this cup tie and become a talking point for weeks. In the end it all revolved around the referee and Taylor's controversial request for him to be switched.

Steve Sims has played well against us but I am sure that every time he jumps with big Niall he fouls him. In the closing minutes we are awarded another free kick and before it is taken I say to the referee: 'Watch Sims, he is climbing all over our number nine.' As soon as they both go for Willow's free kick a linesman flags and we all stop. David O'Leary stands still, Willow waits for the penalty decision to be given and everyone waits except the referee and the Watford players. The ball is switched to our end and Blissett races away to score again. All hell breaks loose. We force the referee to speak to the linesman, still convinced that a penalty will be given. The boss is on the touchline, the crowd are going mad and no one really has a clue what is going on. Then our referee overrules the linesman and we are out of the cup.

At the end of the game there is more emotion, swearing and a confrontation takes place with Taylor. Steve apparently has a go at him although I didn't realise how bad it looked until I saw the incident on television later. Willow doesn't like being cheated and admits that is what he called Taylor and the incident is blown sky high next day in the papers. I have said before that I believe referees have a difficult job to do and the Arsenal versus Watford cup tie was as tough as they come to handle. The spotlight was on Stevens because of Taylor and I am certain now the Football Association should have acted and switched him to another quarter-final. Once Taylor made his comments public Stevens was under pressure.

Once the linesman flagged it had to be a penalty. Was Stevens affected by the pre-match headlines? No one will ever know.

Tempers are high in the dressing-room and the boss just sits in the corner asking everyone if it was a penalty. Willow is going mad with Taylor, the referee, everything. I am disappointed because I have had a poor game and, indirectly, I am responsible for the first two goals. It is a miserable feeling to be out of the cup, especially coming so soon after the celebrating of getting to Wembley, but I am more disappointed with the way I have played and it is all down to my stomach complaint. What is it?

Sunday March 15

A day off and a time to reflect on our worst performance of the season. It was a miserable Sunday.

Monday March 16

The papers are full of how the referee admitted that the linesman did give a penalty but that he overruled him. 'I was five yards away from the incident, my linesman was 50' Stevens is saying. If that is his honest opinion fair enough, all anyone in football asks of the officials is honesty. Training today is carried out with very much of a Watford hangover. The players are still talking about the incident and it is not the ideal preparation for the game against Nottingham Forest tomorrow night.

Tuesday March 17

Arsenal 0 Nottingham Forest 0
We struggled and the Championship is now well and truly blown. At least we didn't concede a goal but we looked tired, jaded and in need of a spark to trigger off all the goods habits of earlier in the season. I wonder just how much those games with Tottenham took out of us.

We didn't create enough chances and the pressure is now back on the boss to sign cover for the first team as players drop out with injury and wrestle with the problems of fatigue and tiredness. It is our first point in the League for three matches and that is a measure of how we are struggling. It is a victory thrown away because Forest are also going through a bad period and, away from home, they should be beaten.

Thursday March 19

The boss called a meeting today and told us that he was resting Viv, David Rocastle and Steve Williams from the match at Watford on Saturday. They are all one booking away from missing the Littlewoods

Martin Hayes tries to find a way past the Watford defence in our controversial FA Cup tie at Highbury.
(Bob Thomas)

Cup Final and he doesn't want to take the risk. None of the players are happy because they want to play, although they can all understand the reason. Rocky looks tired anyway, he has had a long season.

There is also a worry that the Watford game could get out of hand after the controversial cup tie, although I doubt it. Seven days in football is a long time, tempers were high on the day and there is no ill-feeling about Watford in our dressing-room. I must say I don't agree with the rule that if players are booked in the League they miss cup games. I believe that there should be a separate disciplinary system for each competition.

Friday March 20

An article appeared in one of the papers today about Arsenal's wanted list for next season. Players don't take any real notice of speculation like this although I admit that I read it to see if there were any left-backs mentioned. I didn't train much today and had more treatment on the stomach. I have got to keep going because Wembley is rapidly approaching.

Saturday March 21

Watford 2 Arsenal 0

We have now scored just one goal in the last seven First Division matches and that is a true indication of how our performances have dipped. Players seem to have stopped doing what they are good at, we are not creating enough chances and it must be tempting for the boss to criticise. He can't of course because in his first season we have taken Arsenal to a cup final and challenged for the Championship.

There is no question however that we are struggling at the moment. I am sure the boss is looking and learning about life in the top drawer. Charlie played some great stuff today however and I still can't believe that we have lost. Perhaps this is a turning point and the lads are looking forward to a week's holiday in Portugal starting tomorrow. It will be a welcome break, the more so because we are picking up injuries. I am not fit and now Tony Adams has a sinus problem.

Sunday March 22

We flew to Portugal at the crack of dawn and are staying at the same hotel in the Algarve that Elaine and I have visited for our family holiday for the last four years. It is home from home for me and I know the boys will enjoy it. It is a week of relaxing, sunbathing, eating and the odd beer or two! We had a couple of runs, walks and occasional three-a-side games but the boss was not keen for us to work too hard. We spent most of the time by the side of the pool, recharging batteries.

Thursday is transfer deadline day in England and Arsenal are expected to sign a new player. One of the boys bought an English newspaper and the story said that George Graham had flown home to complete a deal. I showed it to the boss who was asleep next to me at the pool! There is, however, something happening back home. I am sure of that.

Thursday March 26

We returned from Portugal to the headline that Alan Smith of Leicester has signed for us in a £700,000 deal which just beat the transfer deadline. I was right, there had been things going on and I later discovered that our chief scout Steve Burtenshaw had done the negotiating while George was away.

I am pleased to see Smith arrive because it increases the strength of the squad. I don't believe that the boss is looking to sell anyone and Smith adds depth to the first team pool. Niall is obviously anxious about Smith coming but I have told him not to worry. Quinny is a good player who has improved tremendously this season and Smith has no divine right to the number nine shirt.

Friday March 27

Only light training and the players are happy and relaxed after the holiday in Portugal. We need a win tomorrow.

Saturday March 28

Arsenal 0 Everton 1
We knew we had to beat Everton to regain confidence, stay with the leaders and keep the fans happy. We should have beaten them and at times they couldn't get a kick but, once again, we failed to score goals.

The boss gets very frustrated, and who can blame him? We haven't scored in our last three League games now and with Wembley coming up it isn't the best of preparation. We work hard in training to create chances and then seem to freeze in matches. I feel a bit sorry for the front players like Quinny and Charlie and they are definitely feeling the pressure.

To make matters worse it was a diabolical goal we gave away. John Lukic cleared straight to Wayne Clarke and although he finished with a great one-touch it should never have happened. We have played both Liverpool and Everton recently and I am definitely tipping Spurs for the title. They have the hardest run-in but are playing the best football and have the strength in depth in their squad to do it.

Sunday March 29

Tony Adams has pulled out of the England squad to play in Belfast on Wednesday and, deep down, I know I should join him. But what can I do? I want to play in the European Championships and the Little-woods Cup Final at Wembley, the biggest game of my club career, is next Sunday. I decide to go and explain my injury situation to Bobby Robson. He understands and agrees to let me miss training tomorrow.

The boss is not happy that an important England international is planned a few days before one of the domestic finals. I have to agree that it is a stupid situation; top players travel all over Europe and then return to play in a Wembley cup final. It is typical of English football however, and we will never change. We complain long and hard and yet next season when clubs have a free Saturday we will no doubt fly off somewhere for a money-spinning exhibition game.

Tuesday March 31

I have played in Belfast a few times and the problems there and the security that surrounds the England party don't worry me any more. We are in safe hands and the Football Association don't allow anything to get in the way of the football. We are here to do a job, nothing else.

Wednesday April 1

Northern Ireland 0 England 2
Scorers: Robson, Waddle
I felt better this morning and felt no reaction to my injury. It was the same during the game and I am pleased that it turned out to be an easy victory for England. Our defence was not placed under pressure and I had no difficult twists, turns or sprints to make.

I don't think I have played against such a poor Irish team. After Chris Waddle and Bryan Robson scored they didn't want to know and the game died during the second half. They just seemed to be happy to keep the score to 2–0. How they miss players like Gerry Armstrong and Sammy McIlroy, players who never give up and who die for their country. The England dressing-room is buzzing now and we feel that we are on our way to the European Championships. If we don't make a muck up of the Turkey game, we should be OK.

1-0 to England. Bryan Robson guides his header past Northern Ireland 'keeper George Dunlop.
(Bob Thomas)

10

WEMBLEY, WEMBLEY

Thursday April 2

It is a day for the Press at our London Colney training ground before the Littlewoods Cup Final. The boss said that he wanted a day when all the interviews could be done, pictures taken, and television items filmed so that we could then be left alone to concentrate on Liverpool. It is fair enough, especially as there are only four days left before we go to Wembley.

The boss named his team and it is the side that everyone expected with Michael Thomas and Perry Groves as the two substitutes. Ian Allinson is disappointed, especially after getting the crucial equaliser against Spurs in the semi-final replay but the boss likes Perrry's pace and he is certain to get on if things are tight on Sunday.

While away with England this week I was asked to comment on reports that Charlie could be leaving Highbury. His contract is up at the end of the season and there is speculation that he may go, or not be offered a new contract. I don't know the exact details although I am happy to make a plea for Charlie to stay. There is no substitute for class, especially up front, and I would be sorry to see a popular figure, who also happens to be a good player, leave. 'Don't go Charlie' the headlines said and that is about right.

All teams when they get to Wembley have a cup final pool, a system that collects money for personal interviews, special pictures or television appearances. Ours is run by Eric Hall, who also acts as an agent for a lot players in football including Rixy and me. Eric is an ideal man for the job because he is only interested in what is best for the players. He wants to make us as much money as possible without upsetting anyone. He works hard at it too and is never off the telephone, organising this and telling me that I have got to be at a certain place for an interview. He is my agent, although we don't have a contract signed – only a gentlemen's agreement. If he puts together a promotion for me he takes a percentage and it works well. It takes the pressure of 'phone calls and the organisation of events off my shoulders.

Opposite: Farmer Sansom and the boys preparing for Wembley. Fortunately, our regular transport was on hand to take us to the Littlewoods Cup Final . . .
(Doug Poole)

Friday April 3

It is time to concentrate on Liverpool and we went over the recent League game against them. The idea is to close them down in midfield as much as possible and put pressure on Ronnie Whelan, who is playing as a makeshift left-back. It is vital that Martin Hayes and Rocky take it in turns to try and force him into mistakes.

Saturday April 4

On Thursday I could hardly walk and today thankfully my stomach feels better. It is not right but nothing is going to stop me walking up that tunnel tomorrow afternoon. The adrenalin is pumping through

Opposite: 'You see, it's
like this Kenny . . .'
(Bob Thomas)

my body already. We didn't do much training, only a few free kicks
and set pieces and my mind is now firmly set on one thing, lifting that
trophy above my head at the top of those steps. I have thought about
this since I was a kid and want it badly.

We checked into the Noke again tonight and it has become our lucky
hotel; we have never lost a match after staying overnight there. OK,
we lost the first leg of the semi-final against Spurs but we still got to
Wembley. The lads are confident, and though our recent form
suggests that Liverpool will win, deep down I think it is going to be
Arsenal to celebrate in their centenary year.

Sunday April 5

Liverpool 1 Arsenal 2
Littlewoods Cup Final
Scorer: Nicholas (2)
It is the buzzer sounding in the dressing-room telling you to line up
outside the door in the tunnel that hits you the most. You know now
that there is no turning back. I have always wanted to play at Wembley
for my club side, always wanted to be a winner, and suddenly this is it.
The drive from the Noke, down Wembley way, the red and white of
our supporters is forgotten. Steve Williams is making a video of the
entire day – leaving the hotel, the coach journey, the preparations in
the dressing-room – and I hope that it doesn't pick up the tension in
my face. Because it is there, I can feel it.

Outside the dressing-room it is a hubbub of anticipation. Come on
Kenny, you have been here so many times before with England, you
must be used to it by now. But somehow this is different. I am nervous,
really nervous. There is Molby, and McMahon. The boss likes those
two and we must not allow them space to carry the game to us. Where
is Rushy? Oh forget it, he will turn up sooner or later.

The boss has a plan of where we are to stand and it is going to be
slightly different from the usual Wembley routine today because the
guest of honour, Sir John Moores, is too ill to walk far and so we must
line up and stroll over to him before shaking hands. The atmosphere
when you walk out into the sunlight is fantastic. You blink and look
and think. It is 'Boys' Own' stuff and I want this to go on forever.

We have been told the first 20 minutes are going to be vital because if
Liverpool get hold of you then, they never let go. And they have
started well, we can't get a kick and we are under pressure. This is not
going as planned. Then they score and I feel sick from my stomach. It
is Rushy, it has to be Rushy. Liverpool have never lost a game when
Ian scores a goal and that goes through all our minds. What are we
going to do? We need some inspiration from somewhere and I decide
that someone has got to go on a few runs to try and take the game to
Liverpool. A couple of times I ended up on the halfway line in an effort
to lift the tension from our play. The boss told me off at half-time but I

The nerves show as we
line up before the kick-off.
(Doug Poole)

told him that someone had to be seen to be doing something. 'I will do the same again if necessary' I said and meant it.

Then we scored and any nerves suddenly lifted. The moment Charlie got his first I knew that we would win the match. Before the final we had not played well for weeks and that reflected in our early play. Now suddenly Willow wanted the ball again, Rocky was involved and Paul Davis started to spray passes around. It clicked together like it did earlier in the season.

When Liverpool kicked off to restart after Charlie's goal I told myself to enjoy the rest of the match. 'If you don't enjoy this, you won't enjoy anything in your life' I repeated to myself. I could see that we were getting stronger and that some experienced Liverpool players looked tired and strained. I shouted instructions, did everything I could to

Charlie's second goal beats Bruce Grobbelaar – the cue for Perry to go into orbit.
(Doug Poole)

make us score a winner. There are times in a football match when you don't have a clue how long there is to go.

Perry came on and started to use his speed, obviously under instructions. And then it happened, the goal I will remember for the rest of my life. It wasn't a great goal but I can still see it now crossing the line in front of a bank of red and white support. Charlie disappeared under a human mountain and I went beserk. I danced, jumped, punched the air and did everything I could to release the pleasure.

How long to go? I remember Venison fouling me, and hearing myself asking the referee Lester Shapter how many minutes left. 'Five' he said and it seemed like a lifetime. Where is Rushy? Surely he can't rob us of this moment? The whistle, that lovely noise, Liverpool droop, we jump and Arsenal have won the Littlewoods Cup in their centenary year with me as captain. I never thought I was a winner and here I am in the middle of Wembley jumping on someone's back and shouting. It is great, incredible. How do I describe this when a million things flash through your mind in seconds? Everyone is rushing around saying 'You little beauty', the boss's favourite saying.

In those ten or fifteen minutes when I had to collect the cup I would have done or said anything. That is how it gripped me. I couldn't wait to get up those stairs and get my hands on the trophy. I wasn't

Opposite: Hello Mum!
(Doug Poole)

bothered about the medal, I wanted the cup. As a kid I had watched on television as people like Emlyn Hughes lifted the cups for Liverpool and his face always told the story of happiness. That is what I wanted. The lads said I couldn't wait to get up the stairs and they were right. Someone stuck an Arsenal hat on my head and I was later criticised for wearing it when I was handed the trophy. I hope no one was offended and there is nothing I can do about it now, it is there in the pictures for everyone to see.

In recent years Liverpool had sung 'Here we go' in front of the photographers and we were determined to have a go at that. Charlie was singing and it is good to see the boss so happy. What a great first season in charge for him. There is Elaine in the crowd, she looks elated, and why not? I was told later that she went berserk on the coach travelling away from the stadium and that reflects just how much this meant to me. She knew.

It is difficult to describe the dressing-room; it is like the inside of one of those parties you wished you hadn't visited. Bottles everywhere, kit strewn around and Paul Merson taking the film with Steve Williams' video. This is the happiest dressing-room I have ever been in, beating the atmosphere after the semi-final victory over Spurs at White Hart Lane.

I sat between Pat Rice, a member of Arsenal's double-winning side, and now the club's youth team coach, and other members of the staff. From the sidelines of the party I watched the happy faces and listened to the things people say when they are intoxicated with success. The champagne corks were a backing group to the singing and it was a marvellous place to be. It meant so much to everyone concerned. It meant more than anything to me – my first cup final, perhaps my only one, and a winners' medal. 'Hey, boss, I have never lost in a final, you know!' I shouted. I don't think he heard me. It didn't matter because everyone was talking at the same time. Directors came and went, the chairman popped in, Theo was covered in champagne and the lads were doing things that I would never remind them of.

The cup was passed around, filled to the brim with champagne. It tasted like the greatest drink in the world. I wondered what the atmosphere in the dressing-room across the tunnel was like. Liverpool were the favourites, Ian Rush had been set to say goodbye in style before he leaves for Juventus. But this was our day; perhaps, in the club's centenary year, it was meant to be.

We wanted the party to go on for ever. What a shame that there are League matches to come and what a fantastic feeling it must be to win the FA Cup when the season is over. What the hell, let's enjoy the moment. We all went, players, staff and their wives and girlfriends, to a restaurant for a party that had been organised by Rixy. We got there about 7.30 pm and the wives arrived, as high as kites, about an hour later.

The perfect finish to a great day. Tony Adams receives the PFA's Young Player of the Year Award.
(Bob Thomas)

Viv, David Rocastle, me and Tony Adams, who had to collect the Young Player of the Year award, had to leave the fun and take a taxi to the Professional Footballers Association Dinner to receive our prizes. I am extremely proud that I have never missed a season as the left-back selected for the PFA's divisional awards. That is two in the Third Division, two in the Second and six in the First!

By the time we returned it was gone midnight and you can imagine the state we were in – we were all drunk, that lovely feeling when you have achieved something in your life and you want to celebrate. It is good to see the boss letting himself go. George Graham isn't a man to drop his guard in public and yet here he is, celebrating in style. I can still see his face when our second goal went in, a huge smile, his eyes alight with the prospect of glory. Tonight he is totally relaxed with the air of a man who knows he is a winner.

And so to bed. And so to sweet dreams, dreams of seeing Charlie's goals go in, dreams of referee Lester Shapter blowing his final whistle, dreams of the biggest party in my career. You couldn't have written a better script for this great club. Arsenal's centenary year and a trophy in a new manager's first season. It's fairytale stuff and I have a hunch that it will be the first of many trophies for George Graham.

11

A PROBLEM SOLVED, A PROBLEM FOUND

Monday April 6	I do remember waking up, with a hangover. Thank God it is a day off. When I can focus it is wonderful to read the headlines. Arsenal winners. Kenny Sansom a winner, I never thought the day would come.
Tuesday April 7	The boss called me into his office today and I am being rested against West Ham tomorrow night. I am not too disappointed, there is no question that I need a break. The injury, whatever it is, does affect my play. I am not as fit and I am not the same player.
	I have also been sent to see a heart specialist following my admission in the *Sun* about my hereditary heart complaint. The club's insurance company wants reassurance about my fitness and today I went to a clinic for a series of tests. To my relief the doctor who carried out the tests said he was staggered how fit I am. I started with an 18-minute run on a treadmill and all the tests I had to do I passed with flying colours. I could have told the doc it is not my heart I am worried about but my stomach.
Wednesday April 8	West Ham 3 Arsenal 0
	I must be the world's worst spectator and I asked the boss if I could skip the game. I am glad I did when I heard the result. There must have been a reaction from the cup final although I know that the boss will not be happy.
Thursday April 9	In for treatment today and I got the lowdown about last night from our physio, Gary Lewin. I had read in the morning papers about the game and the fact that the boss said that he could never allow a similar performance and knew that you could double his disappointment. Gary confirmed how badly we had played, and how disappointed the boss had been.
	The boss will not tolerate a dip in attitude and yet it is impossible to slag the side off. A few days earlier we won the Littlewoods Cup and this season has been one long slog for the players, especially the young ones. We have played so many games and George has got to take

everything into consideration before he starts to say things he may regret. I don't want to make excuses and yet I find it easy to say: 'Be easy on the youngsters, boss.'

A story has appeared in the *Daily Mail* that I am out for the rest of the season because of my stomach strain. The story couldn't be further from the truth because I intend to go on playing at least until England's next European Championship match in Turkey. I have spoken to the boss about my problem many times and the fact remains that I still don't know what is causing the discomfort.

Friday April 10

Trained for the first time this week and I intend to play against Charlton tomorrow. It should be a great occasion because we are going to parade the cup in front of the fans at Highbury.

Saturday April 11

Arsenal 2 Charlton 1
Scorers: Hayes (penalty), own goal.
There is a buzz about Highbury today and the cup gives the match an extra boost. The game starts superbly with the boss and I walking out holding the cup through a tunnel of Arsenal players. The fans go mad and even the Charlton supporters give us a standing ovation as our lap of honour gets to their end. The memories of a week ago come flooding back and this really does mean a lot to the Arsenal fans. It is great to be involved with a winning set-up at last.

Charlton are no real problem. We have played them three times now this season and they have all been similar games. They are in relegation trouble and though it is hard to get really motivated at this time of the season when there is nothing to play for except respect and pride, I never feel we are going to lose the game.

It is FA Cup semi-final day and Spurs are playing Watford. It would be nice if they lost so we could be the only North London winners but I am not too bothered.

Monday April 13

At last, a breakthrough with my injury. I visited top specialist Nigel Harris this afternoon and, after examining me, he thinks I may have a hernia. I have been given a letter to see another doctor and it looks as though my season could be coming to an end.

Tuesday April 14

Arsenal 0 Newcastle 1
This was a bitterly disappointing performance. I watched from the stand and it seems as if the lads have had enough. We have won a trophy and the season is in danger of falling away completely. There were times when we didn't try, and it is a very difficult time for the boss. He is extremely upset at our recent League displays and yet what can he do about it? The lads are not motivated and the boss is undecided what to do. Does he criticise us or does he let it go and wait until next season?

I know that he is desperately keen not to allow the season to die out. He has got to coax the last little effort out of a bunch of players who are struggling to lift themselves. We have been called into training tomorrow and that is significant. It is a good move by the boss because he can't be seen to be allowing the season to drift away.

Thursday April 16

In for training and I have plotted my Easter programme. I am not playing against Wimbledon on Saturday but will face Leicester on Monday at Highbury and then see the specialist the next morning. It is a good idea because the injury is always really sore after matches and that is the perfect time to be examined. In a way I am looking forward to it because at last I will discover what is wrong.

Saturday April 18

Wimbledon 1 Arsenal 2
Scorers: Davis, Merson.
I got more stick from the lads yesterday because I am not playing against Wimbledon. They call me the 'home' captain these days, with Paul Davis leading the side when I don't play. I asked the boss if I could miss the game and go to the wedding of my niece. I do hate watching Arsenal play when I want to be involved myself.

When we came out of the church an uncle told me that Wimbledon had beaten us 2–1 and it wasn't until I was driving to the reception and turned on the car radio that I heard the correct score. It is a great result because Wimbledon are a tough nut to crack at Plough Lane especially because their manager Dave Bassett has told us how he likes to beat the 'big boys' in the First Division.

We had slaughtered them at home and this is a good 'double' for the lads. I later discovered just how well our young centre-forward Paul Merson had done on his full debut and we now seem to be well off for strikers. We have Charlie, Martin Hayes, Quinny, new signing Alan Smith, Perry Groves and young Paul and they are all players who can go down the middle. There have been periods this season when we have struggled to score goals but the options are wide open now. David O'Leary told me how well Paul had played, how he never stopped, hustled people, held play up and got on the end of everything. I am pleased for him because he is a fine young prospect and I know the club rate him highly.

Sunday April 19

In to Highbury for treatment, and Quinny is with me in the treatment room. He has an ankle injury and feels fed up with life. Smith is in the background for him and his season is ending on the wrong note. But I have told Quinny many times how highly I rate him and I'm sure he will be a key member of Arsenal's plans next season.

Monday April 20

Arsenal 4 Leicester 1
Scorers: Hayes 2, Davis, Nicholas
A big day for Alan Smith and it was strange to see our new signing running out for Leicester this morning. Arsenal agreed to let Smith stay at Filbert Street until the end of the season and help their relegation battle, but it didn't stop our fans chanting his name and getting a wave back. I feel a bit sorry for the Leicester supporters because they know they are losing their best player, whatever happens to them. Though we are too determined and skilful for Leicester, Smith proves what a class player he is. He is comfortable on

Tossing up with Leicester City captain Ian Wilson before my last Arsenal appearance of 1986-87.
(Doug Poole)

Opposite: David O'Leary keeps an eye on Gunner-to-be Alan Smith.
(Doug Poole)

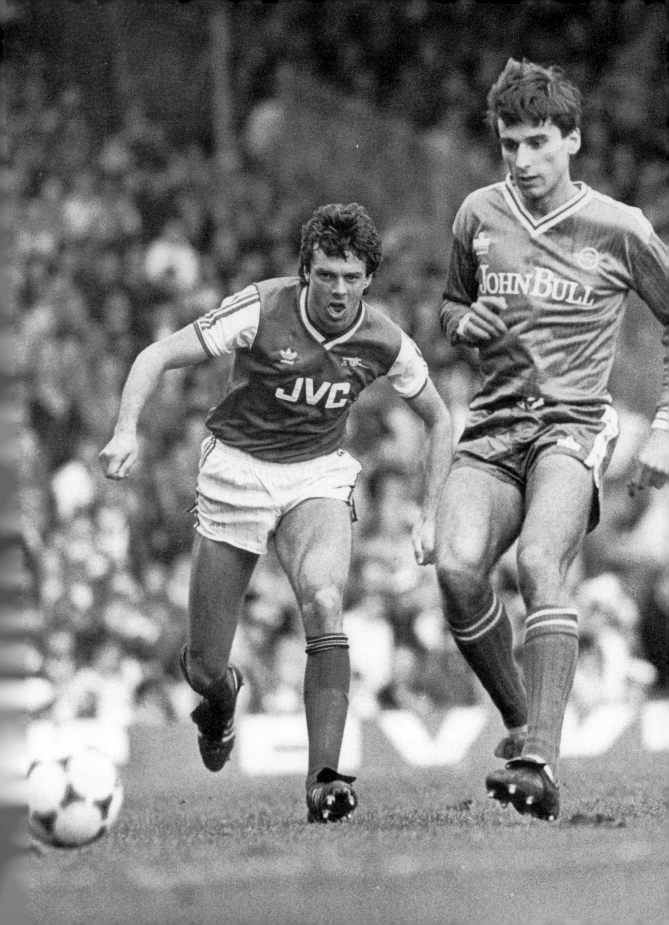

the ball, holds it up well, good in the air and has pace. I am certain he will slot in well next season.

We scored two great goals this morning, the first a wonderful solo effort from Martin Hayes that began with him running on the halfway line and running through the Leicester defence to score and take him over 20 goals for the season. That is a brilliant achievement for a young player who was not first choice until after the season started. Charlie got the other with a superb curling angled shot after I had gone on an overlap. It doesn't look as though I am going to score this season! One a season would do me but matches and time are running out.

I don't mind morning kick-offs. The atmosphere is different and it allows you to get home early for more time with the family.

Tuesday April 21

The day of reckoning. My injury is sore and I am pleased that I am seeing a specialist, someone called Gilmore. As I travel to his office I pray that he discovers just what has been troubling me all these weeks. It doesn't take him long to confirm that I have a hernia. 'I will book you in straight away for an operation' he says. I am relieved to know but I explain that I really want to play against Turkey in Ismir next week and after a further examination he agrees that I can.

I need an operation, and in a way I am looking forward to it. It seems that I have been playing for weeks with a hernia and the exercises I have done have obviously aggravated the injury. I would say that I have been 20 per cent less effective in recent weeks. It has cut down on my pace, dented my confidence and I have had to use all my experience to get through matches. However I don't believe that I have been exposed too badly. There were the two goals against Watford but I have never finished a game thinking that I have played really badly. There were times when I had to gee myself up before the kick-off to blank out the pain and the thought of being beaten for pace and it is amazing how long I have continued playing with such an injury. So, there it is, I have played my last game for Arsenal this season and the greatest year of my career is almost over.

It began way back at the start of last summer when I reported for World Cup duty with England. A year of hope and glory began and it is incredible how much has been packed into that time. World Cup despair, hope and then terrible disappointment, a new club manager, a disappointing start to the season, a wonderful run of 22 matches unbeaten and, finally a trophy for the first time. It has been a year of wonderful memories. The boss has been great and when I told him that I needed an operation but wanted to play for England he agreed straight away.

Wednesday April 22

The *Sun* is running a back page story this morning that I am to be sold by Arsenal. I hadn't seen it until I walked into the dressing-room at Highbury and the lads started to ask me where I was going and saying that I had kept it quiet. It is news to me and the boss says he doesn't know anything about it either when I confront him with the newspaper. He says that the story is untrue and he has no intention of letting me go. It is reassuring to hear although these things do put doubts in your mind.

All I can do is believe George Graham. I know that I haven't been at my best for a few weeks and the story says that Arsenal could cash in on me and buy Nigel Winterburn of Wimbledon. But I have no ambition to leave Highbury – I love it here and want to sign a new contract in the summer.

Thursday April 23

I am now just going through the motions to retain some level of fitness for the England game. Nothing strenuous, just a little jogging and some bicycle work. Gary Lewin is keeping an eye on me and it is only a question of being sensible for next Wednesday.

Saturday April 25

Manchester City 3 Arsenal 0
The boss allows me to stay behind and Elaine and I have invited a few friends around for a barbecue. It is a nice day and I just want to relax – though I keep in touch with the football scores on teletext and can't believe it when City keep scoring. They are a poor side and this only makes me want to play. I know the boss will be bitterly disappointed in going down to a side who are almost certain to be relegated. To me it is a clear indication that the lads have had enough and only want to get the season out of the way. It sounds like a tired performance.

Sunday April 26

The start of my last active week of the season and the plan is the normal England routine. Report to HQ by 6pm.

Monday April 27

The week starts badly with a two hour delay at Luton while we wait for the plane to arrive from Gatwick. There is fog down there and the last thing we need is to sit around an airport lobby waiting for a long four hour flight.

I started to chat with Don Howe and told him how, for the first time in my career, I needed a break from football. 'I am tired out Don, mentally and physically tired out.' All I want to do is forget about football, lie on a beach somewhere and play with the kids. I suppose it is the pressure of non-stop football. I haven't had a break for years. Two World Cups, tours to South America, the disappointment of failure in Spain and Mexico – it has all finally caught up with me. I am looking forward to the England game but I am looking forward to resting even more.

Tuesday April 28

Bobby Robson knows the score. I had a chat with him yesterday and he accepts that I can't do all the training but will be fit to play in the game.

Wednesday April 29

Turkey 0 England 0

God I feel great this morning – probably because this is my last game. No pain when I get up, no pain when I do my warm-up exercises and no pain in the game. Incredible. I have been struggling for weeks and today I felt as if I had never had an injury in my life. The boss told me as I walked out onto the pitch: 'Give it everything today, Ken, you can have a rest on Saturday!'

The last time we played in Turkey we won 8–0. None of us expected to repeat that and the boss has warned us that Turkey are a much improved side. And they are – I don't believe even Bobby Robson expected them to be so good. They are really flying.

I enjoyed the match and we are all delighted to get a point. It is definitely a point gained, not one lost. Yugoslavia are going to find it difficult when they come here in the European Championships and Turkey can do us a big favour by beating them. If Yugoslavia do win it is going to be one hell of a game in Belgrade in November in the match which will decide who goes to West Germany for the finals.

A round trip to Turkey is a long way to travel in the space of three days and I would be in favour of flying out on Sunday. It would give

John Barnes weaving his way through the Turkish defence during England's 0-0 draw in Izmir.
(Bob Thomas)

One of the team's biggest advantages was our ability in the air – in this match against Everton, Niall Quinn (**above right**) and Viv Anderson (**right**) prove the point for the attack and the defence. My attempt to outleap Wayne Clarke (**above**) at least shows willing.

Right *Littlewoods Cup semi-final, second leg: making sure Nico Claesen doesn't get to the ball first.*
Below *Martin Hayes, the club's top scorer, glides past the stranded Gary Gillespie.*

Above right *Charlie nips in to stab our equaliser past Bruce Grobbelaar.*
Below right *It's there! Charlie and Tony Adams can hardly believe it.*

Above *Tony Adams challenges the great Ian Rush.*

Right *Parading the trophy before the ecstatic Arsenal fans.*

the players more time to relax and acclimatise. Back in London, Viv, Tony Adams, Chris Woods and I book into the Tower Hill Hotel because in the morning Umbro are unveiling the new England kit and we have been chosen to model it. Another first for yours truly. I have never been a male model before.

Thursday April 30

We have taken a lot of criticism from the papers about our perform-ance in Turkey and I think it is very unjust. It seems that most of the critics went with the idea that Turkey were useless and closed their eyes to the performance the Turks actually produced.

The new England kit is nice, although I am not sure about the collar. At least it is baggy and that will please the England players, especially Glenn, who likes to wear his shirt outside his shorts. Perhaps now he will be able to please Bobby Robson by tucking it in his shorts. The only kit sponsorship I have on my own is with Puma, who supply my boots. I have been with them all my career and wouldn't wear anything else. My contract with them is the one real money-spinning venture I have outside my own contract with Arsenal. The company pay me a certain amount every year to wear their boots and in return they can use my name to advertise the product and for promotion work like opening shops. Most players have the same contract with different manufacturers and it is a good perk of the business.

All my business outside of playing and media work is conducted for me by Ian Lassett, a former schoolmaster of mine and now a personal friend. He acts as an advisor over all business matters and will come with me if I can negotiate a new Arsenal contract during the summer. Eric Hall acts for me on all other aspects, such as interviews and promotional projects. It works well and I am indebted to them both.

I am glad the operation is tomorrow because today I have been very sore. Coughing and laughing is a nightmare.

Friday May 1

I went into the Princess Grace Hospital in London at 11.30am and went under the needle at about 1.45pm. Gary Lewin sat through the operation and all I can remember is someone saying 'goodnight' and drifting off into a peaceful sleep.

I woke up for the first time at 4.30pm and immediately felt as if my stomach was on fire. Elaine and her sister came to visit me but I wasn't much company and just dozed off in front of them. Apparently the operation is a success although the hernia was a lot worse than first expected. A stomach muscle had pulled away from the bone as a result of playing on too long with the injury. I am assured however that I will be fit and well and raring to go when Arsenal report back for pre-season training on July 8.

I can remember Elaine telling me that Manchester United are reported to be interested in buying Viv. They have some hope. Arsenal would never let him go, not after the season he has had.

Saturday May 2

Arsenal 2 Aston Villa 1
Scorer: Hayes 2 (one penalty)
Got up for a walk this morning and had to sit down again quickly, but managed to keep in touch with the score from Highbury via the telephone and my mum's teletext service. I am pleased we won and Martin, it seems, can't stop scoring. I know the boss wants to finish the season as high as possible and he would love to end up above Spurs.

Monday May 4

Queen's Park Rangers 1 Arsenal 4
Scorers: Rix (2), Merson, Hayes
A morning kick-off and what a fantastic result. The lads came in to visit me afterwards and for half an hour it was chaos.

They were full of themselves after winning and Viv didn't stop the whole time. He had a go at my dressing-gown, my pyjamas, ate my fruit and told me to get up because there was nothing wrong with me! He really is an amazing character and must be worth at least ten points a season to us. I can't imagine an Arsenal side without him now, the kids love him.

Gus has broken his nose and David Rocastle tells me he has a virus and should be in bed alongside me. I think however he is just worn out after a fantastic season and the boss has called it a virus to protect him from criticism. Quinny has damaged ankle ligaments and needs a rest and my hospital room is a home for the Arsenal walking wounded, but it is good to see the lads in such good spirits.

Tuesday May 5

Had lunch with Ian today and walked down to a local wine bar. It is good to walk and exercise and the hospital don't mind. I'd rather have a bottle of wine and a sandwich than the hospital lunches and it is good to get out in the fresh air. Elaine and I also go out to dinner in the evening but this time I get a taxi back. I'm on painkillers because the pain from the operation is still causing me some discomfort.

Thursday May 7

Out of hospital and it is good to get back home and start planning the future in my mind. I need to get fit again, have a holiday and start with Arsenal next season refreshed, with my appetite for the game 100 per cent once more.

Saturday May 9

Arsenal 1 Norwich 2
Arsenal's final game of the season and while it is disappointing to lose, it can't hide the fact that this has been a great first season under George Graham. It would have been great to go out on a winning note for the fans but I am sure that they know that there are great things around the corner for Arsenal. The 1986–87 season is only the start of a new exciting era.

We had the club's big Centenary Dinner tonight. I didn't do much dancing and it was an occasion for backslapping, much drinking, congratulations, speeches and predictions for the future. A wonderful way for the entire staff of Arsenal Football Club to end the season.

There is no doubt in my mind that George Graham is a winner. He didn't expect to collect a trophy in his first season and the Littlewoods Cup triumph over Liverpool was a wonderful bonus. He wanted to come into Highbury, assess the strength of the playing staff, build a platform and take off next season. It has gone better than anyone dreamed of and I'm sure that, deep down, George is pleased that we didn't win anything else. How would he have followed a League and cup double in his first season? The boss will have learned a lot from his first season in the top drawer. He will have discovered things he never knew about players, opposition and managers and lessons learned will stick out in his memory, like the Watford tie in the FA Cup and the way some of the younger players fell away at the end of the season.

George Graham and Theo are a good partnership. Theo is the joker and George the straight man. He is the kind of manager that demands respect. He doesn't treat players with an upstairs-downstairs attitude but if the boss walks into the room it goes quiet until he breaks the ice. He treats players like adults and if you are sensible there is no problem. If you take liberties with George Graham however you know you are in for big trouble. He arrived with the right attitude and I knew straight away that Arsenal wasn't going to be too big for him.

When Don Howe brought John Cartwright into the club he didn't obtain the respect of the players and you are on a loser from the word go. John started to order us around, change habits overnight and it was hopeless. The boss is different and his attitude has always been spot on. 'Look this is Arsenal, I want to win things and so do you, let's get it right together.'

There is no question that he will introduce new faces, new ideas and step up discipline and create new ideas. He will be tougher mentally and that will bounce back to us. I think Arsenal will win a lot of trophies under George Graham. As I say, he is a winner.

Frank Stapleton and Liam Brady, two of the greats who have played for Arsenal, have always told me that they will never get the club out of their system. 'Once you play for Arsenal, you never forget them' they both say. I couldn't imagine playing for anyone else. Arsenal are the greatest.

Sunday May 10

The season is over; it is time to relax for the Arsenal players and today we left for a well-earned holiday in Cyprus. The boys are happy and in the mood to enjoy themselves, and who can blame them? It has been a long slog and there is a feeling of satisfaction and relief in the air. I am limping after my operation but the boss wants me to travel with the team to keep the family atmosphere going and a few days in the sun isn't going to do me any harm at all.

We are due to play two games, against Apoel in Nicosia and Omonia on the same ground and Luton are also involved in the four-way tournament. The football however is very relaxed and I don't think competitive play is uppermost in the lads' minds. In the first game, against Apoel, Kevin Keegan guested for the home side and he looked good. He played as if he had never retired and was overjoyed to score the first goal. The game ended 2–2 and had to be decided on penalties. Michael Thomas scored out of the best spot kicks I have ever seen – a hop, kick and a jump and the ball was into the top corner before the goalkeeper moved. He takes them regularly for the reserves like that! We won the shoot-out when one of their players stepped up to take a deciding penalty and before he sent the ball over the bar the rest of the team were walking away. 'He always misses' they said.

Because Luton and Arsenal won through to the final, the organisers changed the rules and made it a combined finale. The two English clubs split up into one team and took on the best of the locals. I have to say that Alan Smith was absolutely brilliant. The pitch was bumpy and sandy and he really looked the business. His control is superb and he was the reason we won the game. I know he probably had more to prove than the rest of the lads put together but he looks good for next season.

Saturday May 16

FA Cup Final day in England and time for Kenny Sansom the book-maker to take over. It was a great day. Sun and swimming in the morning and the match live on the box in the afternoon. Niall and I ran a 'book' and we watched Spurs take on Coventry with the TV sound down and a BBC radio commentary giving us the information. We laid odds of 4–1 on Clive Allen getting the first goal and the lads could bet on anything up to 90 minutes. No one predicted 2–2 but the boss won money on Clive scoring the first goal.

We laid new odds for extra-time and the atmosphere became electric as everyone screamed and shouted for their player or score to come right. We had a few beers and the fact that it was a great game made it even better. The locals must have thought we were mad, screaming and shouting in front of a TV with the sound turned off! Between us Niall and I won £90. Not bad for a smashing afternoon's entertainment and £45 will buy a few drinks tonight! It was one of the best cup finals I have seen and Coventry definitely deserved to win – and I am not just saying that because it was Spurs who lost.

Tuesday May 19

The final farewell of the season. Arsenal 1986–87 finally split up at Heathrow Airport and it is strange to say goodbye to all the lads. I wonder if they will all be back on July 8 when we all report for training. Not long is it! At least there is no summer football this year and it feels great to be free of pressure and travelling. I don't usually meet up with any of the players in leisure time. We are so spread out that it is almost impossible to arrange. It won't be long before we are all together again, planning and hoping for another new season. Another trophy? Who knows?

I am shattered and after playing with the kids I sit down to watch England versus Brazil from Wembley. It is on television and strange to miss my first international for a long time. At least my hernia is improving and I have no doubts that I will be back to my best next season. I really want to prove my fitness in pre-season and play in the Football League centenary celebration game against the Rest of the World on August 8. That will be a great curtain-raiser to the season and I hope Bobby Robson picks me.

I enjoyed the Brazil game and thought that Stuart Pearce of Nottingham Forest, who won his first cup as my deputy, did well. You don't get any bigger debut than against Brazil in front of a full house at Wembley.

Wednesday May 20

A bombshell today. The 'phone rang this afternoon and one of the Fleet Street Press boys told me that Arsenal had signed Nigel Winterburn, the Wimbledon left-back for £400,000. I couldn't believe it. I had spoken to George about this only a few weeks ago and he told me he had no intention of selling me or buying a replacement. What is going on? Here am I limping around and Arsenal are signing someone who plays in my position. The 'phone never stops ringing and with every call I get more annoyed. Why didn't the boss tell me? After all, I have just spent a week with him in Cyprus. I probably said too much to the papers and the headlines in tomorrow's papers are sure to be controversial.

A story has also broken that Viv is going to Manchester United. What is going on all of a sudden? We are losing the best right-back in the country and suddenly we have got three left-backs – me, Winterburn and Michael Thomas. Nothing seems to make sense. Do Arsenal want to sell me? I will have to find out in the morning.

Thursday May 21

The headlines in the newspapers were big but I suppose they reflect my frustration. I am annoyed and make my feelings known to the boss when I ring him this morning. I asked George why he didn't treat me like a captain and warn me that he was buying another left-back. 'If you had told me I could have been prepared for the 'phone calls and just told them that Nigel Winterburn was coming as a squad player' I argued down the 'phone. I told the boss that it was my career and living that was in question. 'Am I your captain and left-back, or do you want to sell me?' I asked. 'You certainly haven't paid that amount of money to play him in the reserves.' I honestly felt that we didn't need Winterburn at the club although I accept that he is a fine player.

I hope I put my message across in a sensible way and the boss listened and gave me straight answers. He assured me that my position was not in question, I would be the skipper and first choice at the start of the new season and that Winterburn had been bought as a squad player and nothing else. He argued that Liverpool have a big squad, so why can't Arsenal? In so many words he told me that what he did as manager of Arsenal was was none of my business. Of course, that is right but I just wish he had warned me so that I could have been prepared for the inevitable 'phone calls. It also annoyed me that about six weeks ago Arsenal had denied the story and dismissed it as rubbish.

I certainly don't feel under pressure because I have great faith in my own ability. There is no question, however, that for the first time at Arsenal I have someone challenging me for the left-back spot. Competition is what the boss wants and that is obviously healthy. I just can't help thinking that a right-back is a higher priority than a left-back when you have the England first choice on your books. I saw the boss at Highbury a few days later and we exchanged views again. I know that he was cross with me earlier in the season when I didn't warn him about my articles appearing in the *Sun* concerning my heart problem. 'It is 1–1 now' I joked and we remain on the best of terms.

Viv looks as if he is going to United and that is a terrible blow for us after the season he has just had. Highbury will not be the same place without him. Why didn't Arsenal offer him a new contract earlier? I know that Viv would have signed it had it been put in front of him when he was concentrating on his football. Maybe Arsenal didn't want him any more, maybe they are not sorry to see him go. If there is one thing about George Graham, he does know what he is doing. You certainly can't blame Viv for signing a four-year contract with Manchester United at the age of 30. It is a great move for him.

Who is going to play right-back next season? Michael Thomas has done it in the reserves although I prefer him in midfield. I could do it but I would rather switch to midfield if I moved from left-back. My guess is that the boss will buy someone else.

Saturday May 22

England have been in Scotland since Wednesday preparing for this afternoon's match and it has been strange not to be with them. I can't say I am envious because I made up my mind some time ago that I need a rest, but England weeks are special.

I certainly didn't miss playing in the game at Hampden and from my seat in front of the television it looked a disappointing match. It is not surprising because the players are all tired and jaded after a long season and there is not much in this game at the end of the winter. Players are looking for a rest. The only one who looked really good was Charlie when he came on in the second half for Scotland. Charlie is still in the middle of new contract talks with the boss and all the players hope he stays.

Pearce did well again and he looks to have found himself a place in the England squad. The other left-back I have admired during this season has been Tony Dorigo of Aston Villa. Now he has signed for Chelsea here in London so he should get a bigger stage and is definitely one to watch in the future.

My plans now are to have a week's holiday with Elaine on our own. She deserves it and hasn't had time to sit down for five minutes since Harry was born. Then we will go away for two weeks with the kids to Portugal to our usual hotel. Every year we have to take the girls out of school because by the time they break up Arsenal are back in training.

Tuesday May 26

Popped into Highbury for a sauna and some jogging. The hernia is clearing up all the time. Bumped into Tony Adams who missed the Scotland international with a slight shoulder injury. He said that the pitch was terrible and it was a bad game. Tony confirmed that Charlie was the sharpest player on the pitch.

I plan to play tennis every day on holiday to build up my fitness and make sure there is no problem with the hernia. Then when we get back I will start training four days before the other lads return from their summer break. It is going to be a tough pre-season for me because I have never had an injury like this before. I am still 80 per cent fit but that last 20 per cent has got to be right and allow me to peak at the right time.

Looking back, it has been a great year in my life. Twelve months of action-packed events that have represented a really exciting period in my career. I admit that the boss has surprised me; I didn't expect him to be so good or successful. The 1986–87 season has definitely been just a stepping stone into a new era for the club under George Graham. I believe I have got four years left at the top and those four years could be the most successful of my career. I really believe that.

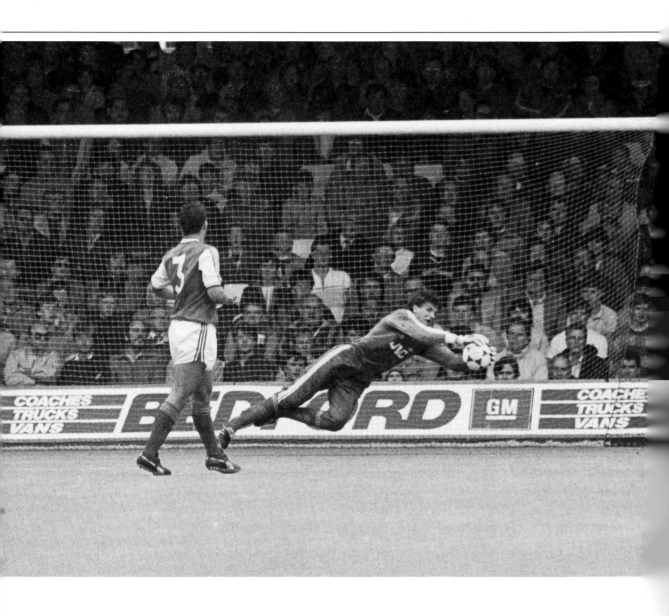

12

ARSENAL 1986–1987

John Lukic John joined Arsenal in the summer of 1983 from Leeds for £50,000 and spent a couple of frustrating years waiting for his chance under the great Pat Jennings. John should be grateful to Don Howe who had great faith in his ability. He made his debut in April 1984 and played 30 games during the 1984–85 season. This season he has really come into his own and played a vital role in our success. The defence was called the mean machine and he was very much one of the team, making vital saves when you most needed them; I particularly remember two from Frank McAvennie in our goalless home draw with West Ham.

He must improve coming out for crosses, and his kicking, but this will mature with confidence. He played throughout the season on a weekly contract and that must have been unsettling. I hope he signs a new long-term contract because he can become a very good goal-keeper. He stood down at the end of the season when the boss looked at our reserve, Rhys Wilmot.

John Lukic
(Doug Poole)

Viv Anderson Viv joined us from Nottingham Forest in July 1984 and seemed to be in the middle of a bad patch. He appeared to be lacking confidence and didn't demand the ball from the goalkeeper enough.

He made up for that this season and 1986–87 must rank as one of the great years of his career. He won his place back in the England team after travelling to two World Cups, in 1982 and 1986, without getting a game, and that is a great achievement at the age of 30. His strengths are many. In the opposing box he wins more headers than their centre-half and scores vital goals. In one against one situations he is as good as any defender in the country and you can't believe his worth in the dressing-room. He is a fantastic team man and the youngsters loved him. We are sorry to lose Viv and Arsenal must have their reasons because you don't let someone like this go without having plans.

Viv's weakness? His left foot. It is only ever used for standing on. A bit like my right one.

Viv Anderson
(All-Sport/David Cannon)

Tony Adams One of Arsenal's great prospects and sure to be a cornerstone of George Graham's era at Highbury. Made his debut at the age of 17 in 1983 and everyone knew then that here was a future England star.

Tony is also tipped to take over the Arsenal captaincy from me although he will have to wait for a few years! He is a born leader and even at his young age has great determination and powers of motivation. Defeat is not in his vocabulary. What a fantastic year he has had. Apart from growing up with Arsenal and winning a Littlewoods Cup medal, he was picked by England for the first time and came through his debut in Spain like a veteran.

He has all the assets. Pace, tackling, is a good header of the ball and has the ability to read situations.

Next season will definitely be harder for him and none of the young lads can expect things to go so smoothly. It is always tougher to live up to reputations. Tony must improve his distribution from the back four. It let us down once or twice when the pressure was on last season and the way Arsenal play we must build and play out of defence.

David O'Leary David is Arsenal's longest-serving player after making his debut in 1975 when he was 17. Everyone was delighted to see him do so well this season because he has had a couple of disappointing years. Injuries didn't help him in that period and he lost confidence.

But David has been through a lot, seen all of Arsenal's successes in the last decade and it was obvious he would come good. The arrival of George Graham obviously gave him a boost and he responded magnificently.

His speed is deceptive and his old head at the back played a big part in Tony's success. David is Arsenal through and through and signed a new contract during the season.

Opposite: Tony Adams
(All-Sport/David Cannon)

Right: David O'Leary
(All-Sport/Michael King)

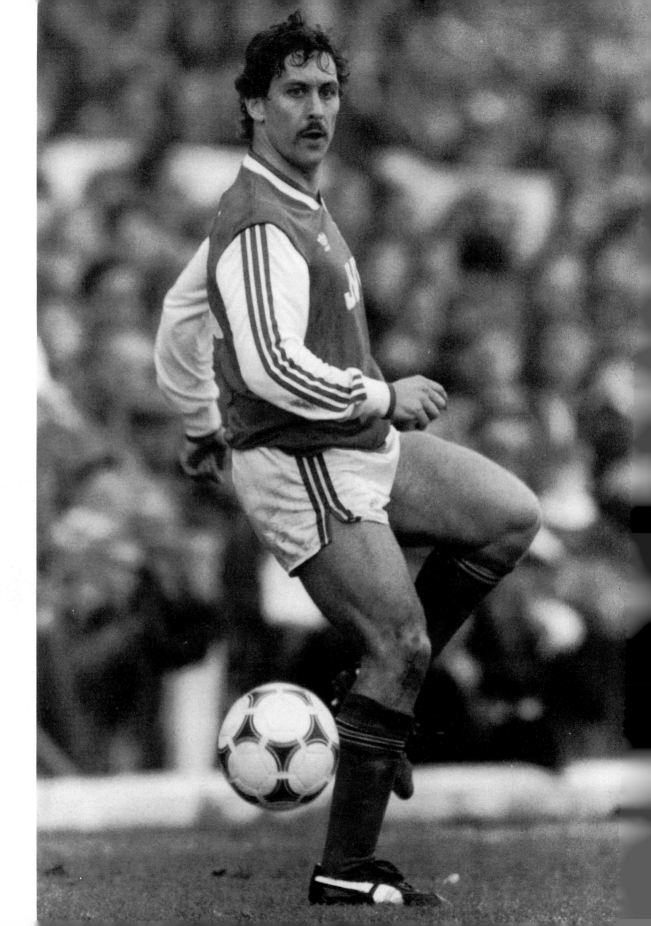

Kenny Sansom The greatest year of my life, but I will play better next season. There is no question that my hernia affected my form towards the end. Technically I can't improve and the only question mark I would put against myself at this stage of my career is getting into the opponents' box more. I would love to score more goals and the lads give me stick over my record.

I have thought about playing in midfield for a couple of years, although that is difficult when you are England's regular left-back and I suppose people will say that my right foot is not strong enough yet it has never worried me.

David Rocastle 'Rocky' is another of Arsenal's men of the future under George Graham. His first full season and what an impact he made. The crowd love him and this young man with great pace and control is going to excite the Highbury faithful for a long time.

He has a lot to learn, of course, like when to take opponents on, when to release the ball, and his heading could improve but all this will come the more games he plays. David must also learn not to react and to control his temper. He got involved with Norman Whiteside at Manchester United and discovered, to his cost, that you can get sent off if you mix it with the big boys.

Arsenal's Player of the Year and he knows that he is going to have to work even harder to win it again – became tired towards the end of the season but a wonderful prospect.

Opposite: Kenny Sansom
(All-Sport/David Cannon)

Right: David Rocastle
(All-Sport/David Cannon)

Steve Williams Another winner. He hates losing and can't tolerate people who don't try or attempt to cheat him. Steve wasn't in the side at the start and then grabbed his chance when Stewart Robson left for West Ham. A very influential player and if he sees a lot of the ball you can bet that Arsenal are playing well.

He joined us from Southampton in December 1984 and this has definitely been his outstanding season so far. I have to keep him under control in certain matches because he can make enemies of referees with his moaning and groaning, but he is a good player to have on your side.

Paul Davis With Viv, my outstanding player of the season. He gained confidence from the arrival of George Graham and his influence spread from the first game. Paul played so well making Steve Williams even more determined and they formed a great double act in the centre of our midfield.

He closes opponents down, tackles well and the only thing he would want to improve on is his passing and heading. Paul must be getting close to a full England cap. Still thinks he is a youngster.

Opposite: Steve Williams
(Bob Thomas)

Below: Paul Davis
(Bob Thomas)

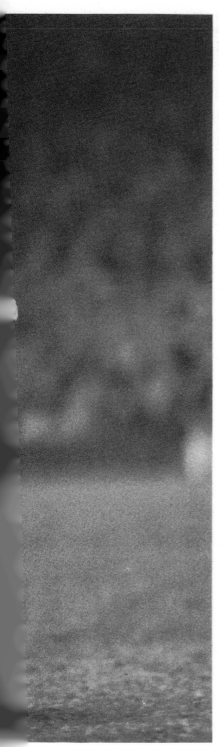

Martin Hayes One of the unexpected success stories of the season, Martin got in after the start and grabbed his chance powerfully. The boss loves pace and Martin has certainly got that. He often wanted to get forward more and we had to hold him back slightly to retain the shape of the side in front of me on the left side. He also likes centre-forward and is the kind of player that allows you to switch tactics and style in the middle of a match.

He doesn't look confident off the field but it comes out as soon as he starts to take people on. He scored some brilliant goals and had the confidence to be our regular penalty taker. But, like the other young-sters, he will find it tough going in the new season. If he scores half of the goals he got this time, Martin will have done well.

Martin Hayes
(All-Sport/Simon Bruty)

Niall Quinn I am a great fan of Niall's and believe he can become a tremendous player. People wrote him off at the start as being too slow and clumsy but he has proved them wrong. His touch has improved, he has two good feet, is great in the air and is learning to use his physical strength.

After scoring on his debut against Liverpool in December 1985 he struggled to make a real impact and then George Graham played him from the word go and he started to believe in himself. Ask the Liverpool defenders or Gary Mabbutt of Spurs just how difficult Niall is to play against.

He was knocked with the arrival of Alan Smith yet Niall should hold his head high and prove that he deserves a place in the side. Quinn v Smith is one of the many battles for places that will take place at Highbury over the next few years under George Graham. He does need more pace and must learn when to 'show' and come for the ball like the great centre-forwards and can learn from Smith. I hope that he fights for his place and doesn't think that he has been replaced and feel sorry for himself.

Opposite: Niall Quinn
(Bob Thomas)

Charlie Nicholas The darling of the Arsenal fans and understandably so. I believe football needs characters like Charlie. If I was a fan I would want to see the unexpected or the bit of ability that gets you off your seat. He has so much skill on the ball. Taking opponents on in their box and scoring goals out of nothing make him a must for most sides.

He has weaknesses, like all players. He doesn't tackle and can be criticised for not following a team pattern. But if you push players like Charlie out of the game, the sport will be the poorer for it. Fans love to see tricks and I'm glad he stayed for the simple reason that Charlie is a matchwinner. Just ask Liverpool in the Littlewoods Cup Final.

Perry Groves George Graham's first signing, Perry has done well. His strength is pace and the fans have taken to his wholehearted approach. He is brave, good in the air and will score goals. Coming from Colchester in the Fourth Division his technique needs to improve but it will come with experience and he is sure to be a vital member of the squad as the boss plots a new era for Arsenal. I saw him grow in confidence as the season progressed.

Opposite: Charlie Nicholas
(All-Sport/Simon Bruty)

Right: Perry Groves
(All-Sport/David Cannon)

Graham Rix Started the season in the side and only an achilles tendon injury robbed him of being part of our success. He is celebrating ten years at Highbury, years in which Graham has not really reached his full potential. He was an England regular during the 1982 World Cup in Spain and was club skipper for two seasons. He takes stick from the crowd and sometimes I can see why he goes for the killer pass. But he is an outstanding player and he and I have a great understanding down the left side of Arsenal's play. I sense he is getting his appetite back and there is no question that he will be determined to be a first choice in the new season. We have still to see a lot more from Graham.

In Cyprus he played left-back and really looked the part. We nicknamed him 'Greg Downs' after the Coventry defender!

Graham Rix
(Doug Poole)

Ian Allinson One of the best goalscorers in the club. He has been given a free transfer now and Stoke have got a bargain. He likes to take people on, is a good crosser and his only problem was that he used to drift out of the game. Many times I told him to get his head up and go look for involvement.

Ian suffered one of the heartbreaks of the season. To score the first goal in the semi-final replay victory at Spurs and then not to be in the Littlewoods Cup Final 13 must have been a bitter pill to swallow. I have asked the boss to try and get some duplicate medals for the lads in the squad who did not get stripped at Wembley.

Ian Allinson
(Doug Poole)

Michael Thomas
(Bob Thomas)

Michael Thomas A young lad who has become a vital member of the squad. Remember how Micky did a great marking job on Glenn Hoddle in the semi-finals, and he prefers to play at left-back! Not another one.

He seems to have more aggression about him in midfield and that is where I prefer to see him play.

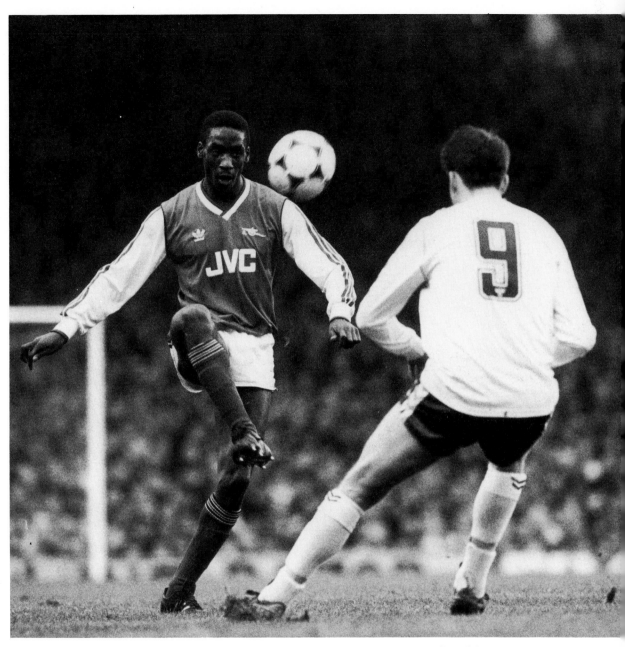

Gus Caesar
(Doug Poole)

Gus Caesar Gus's best position is centre-half and he is one reason why the boss allowed Tommy Caton to leave the club. A good marker and he also found himself in midfield this season. A valuable player.

Paul Merson
(Doug Poole)

Paul Merson This lad is going to be a star. He is quick, keen to learn, has good control and scores goals. When his chance came towards the end of the season, he showed us what he could do with impressive performances. He will be pushing Alan Smith and Niall Quinn for the centre-forward slot in 1987–88.

THE 1986-87 RECORD

DATE	OPPONENTS	F A	ATT	POS.	TEAM (Goalscorers shown in bold type)			
Aug. 23	**Manchester United**	1-0	41,382	–	Lukic	Anderson	Sansom	Robson
Aug. 26	Coventry City	1-2	11,187	–	Lukic	Anderson[1]	Sansom	Robson
Aug. 30	Liverpool	1-2	38,637	16	Lukic	Anderson	Sansom	Robson†
Sept. 2	**Sheffield Wednesday**	2-0	20,101	9	Lukic	Anderson	Sansom	Robson
Sept. 6	**Tottenham Hotspur**	0-0	44,707	11	Lukic	Anderson	Sansom	Robson
Sept. 13	Luton Town	0-0	9,876	10	Lukic	Anderson	Sansom	Williams
Sept. 20	**Oxford United**	0-0	20,676	12	Lukic	Anderson	Sansom	Williams
Sept. 23	**Huddersfield Town** (LC2 1L)	2-0	15,194	–	Lukic	Anderson	Sansom	Williams
Sept. 27	Nottingham Forest	0-1	25,371	15	Lukic	Anderson	Sansom	Williams
Oct. 4	Everton	1-0	30,007	12	Lukic	Anderson	Sansom	**Williams**[1]
Oct. 7	Huddersfield Town (LC2 2L)	1-1	8,713	–	Lukic	Anderson	Sansom	Williams
Oct. 11	**Watford**	3-1	24,076	8	Lukic	Anderson	Sansom	Williams
Oct. 18	Newcastle United	2-1	22,368	7	Lukic	Anderson[1]	Sansom	**Williams**[1]
Oct. 25	**Chelsea**	3-1	32,990	4	Lukic	Anderson	Sansom	Williams
Oct. 28	**Manchester City** (LC3)	3-1	21,604	–	Lukic	Anderson	Sansom	Williams
Nov. 1	Charlton Athletic	2-0	19,614	2	Lukic	Anderson	Sansom	Williams
Nov. 8	**West Ham United**	0-0	36,084	3	Lukic	Anderson	Sansom	Williams
Nov. 15	Southampton	4-0	18,726	1	Lukic	Anderson[1]	Sansom	Williams
Nov. 18	**Charlton Athletic** (LC4)	*2-0	28,301	–	Lukic	Anderson	Sansom	Williams
Nov. 22	**Manchester City**	3-0	29,009	1	Lukic	Anderson[1]	Sansom	Williams
Nov. 29	Aston Villa	*4-0	21,658	1	Lukic	Anderson	Sansom	Williams
Dec. 6	**Queens Park Rangers**	3-1	34,049	1	Lukic	Anderson	Sansom	Williams
Dec. 13	Norwich City	1-1	21,409	1	Lukic	Anderson	Sansom	Williams
Dec. 20	**Luton Town**	3-0	28,217	1	Lukic	Anderson	Sansom	Williams
Dec. 26	Leicester City	1-1	19,205	1	Lukic	Anderson	Sansom	Williams
Dec. 27	**Southampton**	1-0	38,138	1	Lukic	Anderson	Sansom	Williams
Jan. 1	**Wimbledon**	3-1	36,144	1	Lukic	Anderson	Sansom	Williams
Jan. 4	Tottenham Hotspur	2-1	37,723	1	Lukic	Anderson	Sansom	Williams
Jan. 10	Reading (FAC3)	3-1	16,822	–	Lukic	Anderson	Sansom	Williams
Jan. 18	**Coventry City**	0-0	17,561	1	Lukic	Anderson	Sansom	Williams
Jan. 21	**Nottingham Forest** (LC5)	2-0	38,617	–	Lukic	Anderson	Sansom	Williams
Jan. 24	Manchester United	0-2	51,367	1	Lukic	Anderson	Sansom	Williams
Jan. 31	**Plymouth Argyle** (FAC4)	6-1	39,029	–	Lukic	Anderson[2]	Sansom	Williams
Feb. 8	**Tottenham H** (LCSF 1L)	0-1	41,306	–	Lukic	Caesar†	Sansom	Williams
Feb. 14	Sheffield Wednesday	1-1	24,792	2	Lukic	Thomas	Sansom	Williams†
Feb. 21	**Barnsley** (FAC5)	2-0	28,302	–	Lukic	Anderson	Sansom	Allinson†
Feb. 25	Oxford United	0-0	13,296	2	Lukic	Anderson	Sansom	Thomas
Mar. 1	Tottenham H (LCSF 2L)	2-1	37,099	–	Lukic	Anderson[1]	Sansom	Thomas
Mar. 4	Tottenham H (LCSFR)	2-1	41,005	–	Lukic	Anderson	Sansom	Thomas
Mar. 7	Chelsea	0-1	29,301	3	Lukic	Anderson	Sansom	Thomas
Mar. 10	**Liverpool**	0-1	47,777	3	Lukic	Anderson	Sansom	Thomas
Mar. 14	**Watford** (FAC6)	1-3	43,276	–	Lukic	Anderson	Sansom	Williams
Mar. 17	**Nottingham Forest**	0-0	18,352	3	Lukic	Anderson	Sansom	Williams
Mar. 21	Watford	0-2	18,172	3	Lukic	Caesar	Sansom	Thomas
Mar. 28	**Everton**	0-1	36,218	4	Lukic	Anderson	Sansom	Williams
Apr. 5	Liverpool (LCF)	2-1	96,000	–	Lukic	Anderson	Sansom	Williams
Apr. 8	West Ham United	1-3	26,174	5	Wilmot	Anderson	Thomas	Williams
Apr. 11	**Charlton Athletic**	2-1	26,111	5	Lukic	Anderson	Sansom	Williams
Apr. 14	**Newcastle United**	0-1	17,353	5	Lukic	Anderson	Thomas	Williams
Apr. 18	Wimbledon	2-1	8,515	5	Lukic	Anderson	Caesar	Williams
Apr. 20	**Leicester City**	4-1	18,767	4	Wilmot	Anderson	Sansom	Williams
Apr. 25	Manchester City	0-3	18,072	4	Wilmot	Anderson	Thomas	Williams
May 2	**Aston Villa**	2-1	18,463	4	Wilmot	Anderson	Thomas	Williams
May 4	Queens Park Rangers	4-1	13,387	4	Wilmot	Anderson	Thomas	Williams
May 9	**Norwich City**	1-2	24,000	9	Wilmot	Anderson	Thomas	Williams
May 16	F.A. Cup Final							

( ) Time Substitute used   †Player substituted
*Own goal   After extra time.

O'Leary	Adams	Rocastle†	Davis	Quinn	**Nicholas**[1]	Rix	Hayes (80)
O'Leary	Adams	Rocastle	Davis	Quinn	Nicholas	Rix†	Hayes (65)
O'Leary	**Adams**[1]	Rocastle	Davis	Quinn	Nicholas	Rix	Williams (78)
O'Leary	**Adams**[1]	Rocastle†	Davis	**Quinn**[1]	Nicholas	Rix	Hayes (74)
O'Leary	Adams	Rocastle†	Davis	Quinn	Nicholas	Rix	Hayes (77)
O'Leary	Adams	Rocastle	Davis	Quinn	Nicholas	Rix	Groves (75)
O'Leary	Adams	Rocastle	Davis	Quinn	Nicholas	Rix†	Groves (64)
O'Leary	Adams	Rocastle	**Davis**[1]	**Quinn**[1]†	Nicholas	Rix	Groves (62)
O'Leary	Adams	Rocastle	Davis	Quinn	Nicholas†	Groves	Alinson (61)
O'Leary	Adams	Rocastle	Davis	Quinn	Allinson	Groves†	Caesar (85)
O'Leary	Adams	Rocastle	Davis	Quinn	Allinson†	Groves	**Hayes**[1] (55)
O'Leary†	Adams	Rocastle	Davis	**Quinn**[1]	**Groves**[1]	**Hayes**[1]p	Allinson (71)
O'Leary	Adams	Rocastle	Davis	Quinn†	Groves	Hayes	Caesar (88)
O'Leary	Adams	**Rocastle**[1]	Davis	Quinn†	Groves	**Hayes**[2]p	Allinson (76)
O'Leary	Adams	**Rocastle**[1]	**Davis**[1]	Quinn†	Groves	**Hayes**[1]p	Allinson (81)
O'Leary	**Adams**[1]	Rocastle	Davis	Quinn	Grovest†	**Hayes**[1]	Caesar (84)
O'Leary	Adams	Rocastle	Davis	Quinn	Groves	Hayes	Caesar
O'Leary	Adams	Rocastle†	Davis	**Quinn**[1]	**Groves**[1]	**Hayes**[1]p	Caesar (87)
O'Leary	Adams	Rocastle	Davis	**Quinn**[1]	Groves†	Hayes	Allinson (H/T)
O'Leary	**Adams**[1]	Rocastle	Davis	**Quinn**[1]	Allinson	Hayes	Merson (76)
O'Leary	Adams	**Rocastle**[1]	Davis	Quinn	**Groves**[1]	**Hayes**[1]p	Caesar
O'Leary	Adams	Rocastle	Davis	**Quinn**[1]	Groves†	**Hayes**[2]	Nicholas (78)
O'Leary	Adams	Rocastle	Davis	Quinn	Groves	**Hayes**[1]p	Caesar (85)
O'Leary	**Adams**[1]	Rocastle	Davis	**Quinn**[1]	Groves†	**Hayes**[1]	Nicholas (78)
O'Leary	Adams	Rocastle	Davis	Quinn	Groves†	**Hayes**[1]p	Caesar (70)
O'Leary	Adams	Rocastle	Davis	**Quinn**[1]	Nicholas	Hayes†	Allinson (81)
O'Leary	Adams	Rocastle†	Davis	Quinn	**Nicholas**[2]	**Hayes**[1]p	Allinson (85)
O'Leary	**Adams**[1]	Rocastle	**Davis**[1]	Quinn†	Nicholas	Hayes	Rix (77)
O'Leary	Adams	Rocastle	Davis	Quinn	**Nicholas**[2]	**Hayes**[1]p	Rix/Caesar
O'Leary	Adams	Rocastle	Davis	Quinn	Nicholas	Hayes†	Rix (78)
O'Leary	Adams	Rocastle	Davis	Quinn†	**Nicholas**[1]	**Hayes**[1]	Rix (80)/Caesar
O'Leary	Adams	Rocastle	Davis	Quinn	Nicholas†	Hayes	Caesar (72)
O'Leary	Adams	**Rocastle**[1]	**Davis**[1]	**Quinn**[1]	**Nicholas**[1]	Hayes†	Groves† (78) Ceasar (85)
O'Leary	Adams	Groves	Davis	Quinn	Nicholas†	Hayes	Thomas (83)/Rix (76)
O'Leary	Adams	Groves	Davis	**Quinn**[1]	Rix	Hayes	Allinson (76)
O'Leary	Adams	Rocastle	Davis	Quinn†	Groves	**Hayes**[1]p	Nicholas[1] (63)/Thomas (87)
O'Leary	Adams	Rocastle	Davis	Quinn	Groves†	Hayes	Nicholas (55)
O'Leary	Adams	Rocastle	Davis	**Quinn**[1]	Nicholas†	Hayes	Allinson (105)/Caesar
O'Leary	Adams	**Rocastle**[1]	Davis	Quinn	Nicholas	Hayes	Allinson (70)/Caesar
O'Leary	Adams	Rocastle	Caesar	Quinn	Allinson	Hayes†	Merson (69)
O'Leary	Adams	Rocastle	Groves	Quinn	Allinson	Hayes†	Caesar (86)
O'Leary	Adams	Rocastle	Groves	Quinn	**Allinson**†	Hayes†	Nicholas (64)/Thomas (64)
Caesar	Adams	Rocastle	Groves†	Quinn	Nicholas	Thomas	Allinson (73)
O'Leary	Adams	Allinson	Davis	Quinn†	Nicholas	Hayes	Rix (65)
O'Leary	Adams	Rocastle	Davis	Quinn	Nicholas	Hayes†	Groves (63)
O'Leary	Adams	Rocastle	Davis	Quinn†	**Nicholas**[2]	Hayes†	Groves (72) Thomas (83)
O'Leary	Adams	Rocastle	Davis	Groves	Nicholas	**Hayes**[1]p†	Rix (77)
O'Leary	Adams	Rocastle	**Davis**[1]	Quinn†	Nicholas	**Hayes**	Groves (13)
O'Leary	Adams	Rocastle†	Davis	Groves	Nicholas	Hayes	Rix (52)
O'Leary	Adams	Rocastle†	**Davis**[1]	**Merson**[1]	Nicholas	Rix	Allinson (70)
O'Leary†	Adams	Rocastle†	**Davis**[1]	Merson	**Nicholas**[1]	Rix	Caesar (61)
Caesar	Adams	**Hayes**[2] [1]P	Davis	Merson†	Nicholas	Rix	Allinson (72)
O'Leary	Adams	Hayes	Davis	Quinn†	Nicholas	**Hayes**[2] [1]p	Groves (50)
Caesar	Adams	Rocastle	Davis	**Merson**[1]	Nicholas	**Hayes**[1]	Groves
O'Leary	Adams	**Rix**[2]	Davis	Merson	Nicholas	Rix	Groves (45)

		HOME			Goals		AWAY			Goals		
	P	W	D	L	F	A	W	D	L	F	A	Pts
Everton	42	16	4	1	49	11	10	4	7	27	20	86
Liverpool	42	15	3	3	43	16	8	5	8	28	26	77
Tottenham	42	14	3	4	40	14	7	5	9	29	29	71
Arsenal	42	12	5	4	31	12	8	5	8	27	23	70
Norwich	42	9	10	2	27	20	8	7	6	26	31	68
Wimbledon	42	11	5	5	32	22	8	4	9	25	28	66
Luton	42	14	5	2	29	13	4	7	10	18	32	66
Nottingham Forest	42	12	8	1	36	14	6	3	12	28	37	65
Watford	42	12	5	4	38	20	6	4	11	29	34	63
Coventry	42	14	4	3	35	17	3	8	10	15	28	63
Manchester United	42	13	3	5	38	18	1	11	9	14	27	56
Southampton	42	11	5	5	44	24	3	5	13	25	44	52
Sheffield Wednesday	42	9	7	5	39	24	4	6	11	19	34	52
Chelsea	42	8	6	7	30	30	5	7	9	23	34	52
West Ham	42	10	4	7	33	28	4	6	11	19	39	52
QPR	42	9	7	5	31	27	4	4	13	17	37	50
Newcastle	42	10	4	7	33	29	2	7	12	14	36	47
Oxford	42	8	8	5	30	25	3	5	13	14	44	46
Charlton	42	7	7	7	26	22	4	4	13	19	33	44
Leicester	42	9	7	5	39	24	2	2	17	15	52	42
Manchester City	42	8	6	7	28	24	0	9	12	8	33	39
Aston Villa	42	7	7	7	25	25	1	5	15	20	54	36

(Arsenal first went top on Saturday November 15 when they won 4-0 at Southampton. They stayed there until February when Everton took over after beating Coventry 3-1 at Goodison Park. Arsenal didn't play that day – they were waiting to take on Spurs in the Littlewoods Cup semi-final. And they never regained the leadership.)

Goalscorers: Hayes 24 (12 pens). Quinn 12, Nicholas 11, Anderson 7, Davis 7, Adams 6, Rocastle 5, Groves, Merson 3, Williams, Allinson, Rix 2, og 2.